I0453342

CLUELESS
&WISE

Pregnancy, Postpartum, and
Early Motherhood: Adorable,
Raw, and Taboo

**KRISTEN LILLIAN
RIORDAN**

First Printing: 2023

ISBN 979-888992328-2

www.ayurveda-orlando.com

Book Design: Najdan Mancic, Iskon Design

CONTENTS

INTRODUCTION

No one could have prepared me for what was to come. I had dreamt of becoming a mother for years. My mind was committed to images of infatuated mothers, sleeping infants, and giggling babies. I had conveniently placed all aspects of motherhood that I considered difficult and messy out of my field of vision. Motherhood wasn't going to take me by surprise; I was pregnant for forty weeks. In that time, I read all the books, researched all the products, and nested like a mad woman. Yet, when the baby arrived, and motherhood set in, I quickly realized that I was utterly clueless.

While pregnant, I spent countless hours studying books on pregnancy and parenthood. Truthfully, if I have any regrets up to this point, it was reading all those damn books. Some of the books were wonderful—informative and entertaining. Presumably, the authors had no ill will. But by reading those books, I curated in my imagination a set of ideals and expectations of what was happening, and what would come. It didn't take long for me to realize my expectations were unrealistic. According to the schedule many experts recommended, I wasn't able to get my daughter to sleep at the right times. The way I looked, felt, and slept didn't come close to the aspirations I set for myself based on my reading. *"You'll sleep when the baby sleeps"* was my plan. It's almost laughable how unreal that strategy turned out to be. I was riddled with anxiety and sleep wasn't happening. Despite my best intentions, I found myself lost and frazzled. My daughter is now well over the one-year mark, and I'm happy to report, I am finally rested. You've heard me refer to sleep a couple times already, and you'll continue to hear about it, because during one's first year of motherhood, sleep (and poop) are of the highest importance; therefore, they are discussed readily and frequently.

I'm writing this book not as an expert, but as an imperfect human that is still learning. I want to share the whole truth of motherhood, specifically the less attractive topics that are most often relegated to the file labeled, "don't talk about this stuff." I've made an effort to minimize the saccharine narrative that often accompanies tales of motherhood. Of course, I couldn't avoid the sweet stuff fully— we are, after all, talking about babies. But it is my belief that new moms will benefit most from hearing honest accounts of the real deal; not withholding "taboo topics" like hormonal avalanches, mom-guilt, mom-rage, trials in marriage, a crumbling sense of self, and mental health problems. Not to worry though, it's not all heavy; there's plenty of light content too. Throughout pregnancy and early motherhood, the dark and the light overlap and coexist.

What we see on social media and in pop culture can be so misleading. Very few women are posting selfies of tired, bloodshot eyes, floating in sockets of welled up tears. New moms, myself included, are not guilty of sharing lies; we just tend to share partial truths. Postpartum, I found myself on my phone a lot; arguably, too much. I was googling everything under the sun; *best black out curtains for a nursery, proper pumping practices, what temperature should the room be for baby to sleep?* My mind was spinning one hundred miles an hour. The more time I spent seeking answers, the more overwhelmed and underprepared I felt. Sleep deprived and delirious, I found myself scrolling social media while nursing through the long, lonely hours of the night. I quickly realized that my social media use was doing me a grave disservice. I became disenchanted. I compared the totality of my experience to snippets of gorgeous pictures of blissed-out moms with their babies—*I don't seem to be enjoying motherhood like other moms. Other moms are making this all look so easy and beautiful.* I felt like it was all so difficult, and I was alone in the toughness. I also felt fraudulent because I was perpetuating a false narrative. My social media account appeared to be a gallery of my daughter and I with our happiest faces forward. The joy was magical and authentic. Reality is just far more nuanced.

We don't generally feel alone in happy times. You don't need to read a book on how your heart will be broken open in the best of ways, and how you'll love more and deeper than you've ever loved before. You don't need me to describe, at length, the priceless exuberance and abundant sweetness that comes with having a baby. You're about to experience that for yourself, and it will transform your heart in the most spectacular way. But what might be of use to you, is to hear about the tough stuff. I think there are aspects to motherhood that feel, for most, too vulnerable or shameful to share openly—those are the very same stories that bring me the most comfort. We can all relate to the un-pretty pieces of motherhood. I think the reluctance to discuss our less flattering feelings comes from not wanting to come across as grumbly or fragile. But, as Brené Brown says, "Vulnerability is the core, the heart, center of meaningful human experience," so, I'm willing to go there. I don't know anyone who escapes pregnancy and early motherhood without their fair share of tough stuff. There are too many of us going through this for any of us to feel alone.

Part of this feeling of isolation is caused by the fact that people don't accurately remember the most challenging chapters of motherhood. Talk to anyone over sixty and it's all a pleasant blur. Nature designed it that way. If we remembered how hard the journey of motherhood truly was, we wouldn't feel as eager to do it again. If we had accurate recall of the pain of childbirth, and exhaustion of being a new mom, we'd all stop procreating. Biology gave us selective memory for a reason. In such, we walk away telling expecting mothers, *"There will be hard days, but it's all so precious. Soak it all up, because time flies, and they grow so fast."* This is all true, but it's also incomplete. The early days of new motherhood can be some of the longest, hardest days.

I remember calling my brother when my daughter was just a couple weeks old. I was in duress. My brother has two kids. I figured he'd lived the experience, and hopefully would offer some version of wisdom. He said, "Sis, it's wild—overnight, you stop living 24-hour days. You're living in 3-hour cycles; baby sleeps, drinks milk, gets a diaper change, and aims to sleep again. This repeats eight times a day. It repeats day after day for months. It's boggling." I found the experience of new motherhood to be abruptly disorienting. I was pregnant for nine months, but I became a mother overnight. Don't get me wrong, and I think it'll be blatantly obvious as you read this book, I love my daughter more than anything on earth. And at the same time, I wrestled with nearly every aspect of motherhood.

So, if you find yourself madly in love with your baby, and so grateful to be a mom AND you're struggling because as it turns out, it's not all sprinkles and rainbows—I want you to know that you're not alone. The life of a new mother is riddled with paradoxes; for example, some of the best days are also some of the hardest days. This book is laid out in a series of vignettes on a variety of topics that arise during pregnancy and early motherhood. I have also included several excerpts from the journal I kept during that time—fragmented, messy thoughts that captured the moment in real time. I have chosen to write this book when I'm close enough to the experience to recall what happened, but far enough that I've had time to process and work through some of the difficulties I faced. Full disclosure, had I written this book even six months earlier, it probably would have been dripping with self-loathing and resentment—two very real features of motherhood that I will share because I was not prepared to face them at the time. I am sure when I look back on this book five or ten years from now, I will think, "*Geez, Kristen, suck it up. That was such a wonderful time in your life. What were all those complicated feelings about?*" But that's what time does. I respect that, *time heals all wounds,* as they say. But, when I was expecting, and in the thick of taking care of a tiny person for the first time, I would have found so much comfort in the authentic experiences of a new mom who was still a bit raw, and not yet speaking from a place of blurry memories or pure nostalgia.

DISCLAIMER

This book is not instructional. I am in no position to write a how-to guide. These stories and ideas are not intended to be deterministic or reflective of your unique experiences. There are good reasons why pediatricians say the average age for learning how to walk is anywhere between eight and eighteen months. When it comes to babies, there's a huge range of what is considered normal development. As all babies are different, all moms are different. While the experiences I convey were life-altering for me, I know that they are not extraordinary. Ordinary challenges are meant to be shared. Curl up in camaraderie. Know that as you move through this momentous journey, you are in good company.

CHAPTER 1

Baby Fever

I am one of those people who has always wanted a baby, and who has always dreamed of being a mom. I didn't play with Barbies as a little kid. Instead, I treasured my life-size baby dolls. I liked the realistic ones. I dressed them, wiped their little faces, and rocked them in my arms. My little brother was born when I was almost nine years old. I was convinced he was born exclusively for my entertainment. He was my own real-life baby doll. "I'll take care of him," I'd shout from the halls when it was time for his diaper change or sponge bath. I think my baby fever started to rev up for real when people close to me started to have little ones. My nephew was born when I was in my mid-twenties. I adored his little buddha belly, the way he devoured pickles, and how his first word was 'light'. My niece came when I was in my late twenties. Everyone in my family called her my mini-me. I still relish our resemblance; aunt genes do run strong. My niece, Lucy, catalyzed my baby fever in the most ostensible way. From her arrival on, I vetted every guy I dated through a new lens, *"Would he be a good dad?"*

I met my husband, and father to my little girl about six years later. By our fifth date, my husband, Brian and I had already broached the topic of children. We both wanted them, and while we didn't outwardly express it, we were aware of our ages, and both knew we wanted to become parents sooner rather than later. Historically, I've had issues with my reproductive cycle. There were years where it was irregular, with lots of missed periods. Knowing that I had found the person I wanted to start a family with, I did what I could to protect my reproductive health. I took a couple of

Ayurvedic supplements and made a point to eat well. I started tracking my cycle. Each month, I got out my pencil and noted my cycle dates, as well as the length of my period in my paper planner. I started to pay attention to the physical signs of ovulation. Suffice it to say, I was seriously prepping for pregnancy.

Twenty months later in early autumn, we celebrated our nuptials with a small wedding at the beach. We both mentioned starting a family in our vows. Once married we decided to "stop not trying to have a baby, which is a low-risk, inadvertent way of saying, we started trying. We both presumed the pregnancy wouldn't happen right away. However, a few weeks later, my period didn't come. Filled with anticipation and hope, I took a pregnancy test. I read the results as negative. I felt slightly disappointed, but optimistic that the baby was on its way, and that I would be pregnant soon.

There was a lull in activities the following weekend. With the wedding behind us, we had time to decompress. That Saturday, I randomly grabbed a journal and started writing a letter to my unborn child. It was a peculiar thing to do because there was no child to speak of. I wrote, "You're not here yet, but I can feel your presence. I want you to know how loved you are. Your daddy and I love you so much, and we cannot wait to meet you." A few days later, my period still hadn't started. In addition to that, my breasts felt unprecedentedly tender. I decided to take a second pregnancy test. I WAS PREGNANT! I continued to write in that same journal for well over a year. I chronicled all the highs and lows of my expanding belly and growing baby.

I found out I was pregnant on a Monday. I planned on telling Brian that Friday night. After a long week, I wanted to dance into the living room with the song "Who Dat is My Baby Daddy" playing in the background. Embarrassing—I can be a goofy person. Tuesday afternoon, we passed in the hall; he gave me a hug and said lovingly "Just me and my bride". With his comment derailing my plan, I added, "And your baby." One month into marriage, that's how I told my husband we were having a baby. He couldn't have been happier. I couldn't have been happier. The thing I dreamed of and wanted more than anything on earth was finally coming!

1 Day Pregnant

Letter to My Unborn Daughter

Dear Little One,

You're not here yet, but you might as well be. I see you in every child I meet; in my niece's blue eyes and long lashes that flutter when she blinks, in my friend's newborn who rests on my lap with his eyes closed, and legs bent like a tiny frog perched on my thighs. I see you in the toddler who pushes his toy lawn mower while his dad plows the grass alongside him. Everyone says your heart expands when you meet your baby. I can feel mine ballooning already, and I can't wait. I know you will be smart and funny, and you will be oh so loved. Your dad is going to be great to you. I think his presence in my life is why you've chosen to come to me now. I have wanted you for many, many years. In a way, I'm glad I had to wait so long to meet you. The time has given me space to grow so I can be a better mommy for you…yet far from perfect. You're wise, so you know better than to anticipate perfection.

I appreciate that. I can tell you this, I'll do my absolute best with you. I'll aim to keep my own self-imposed limitations, and the insecurities that ailed me, from affecting you. I want you to know you are boundless. Please know that you are free to live your life as such. There's a saying, 'when the student is ready, the teacher will come.' For all I have learned in my life. I think I'll learn the most from being your mom. I'll teach you things too; like to look both ways before crossing the street, tie your shoes, and always say 'thank you". Your daddy and I will do our best to model kindness, cooperation, and respect. We'll teach you about fun stuff too. To see the world through your eyes promises to be darling. I can feel that already.

I love you.
Love,
Mom

CHAPTER 2

Pregnancy

One of the best parts of having a baby is not being pregnant anymore. I'm always in awe, and some degree of disbelief, when I see the breed of woman who basks in the illusive glow of pregnancy. I felt that glow eluded me. Don't get me wrong; I was ecstatic knowing there was a baby growing inside me. I was elated that I was granted the lucky fortune of getting to conceive and carry my own offspring. I loved my daughter when she was a just a speck, a little cell—even before she had a heartbeat. I just didn't have the same affection for the nausea that came in waves all day, every day, for sixteen long weeks. I slept with a stack of saltines next to my bed. I couldn't pep talk myself out of the fatigue. Who knew being tired was so exhausting? My poor husband was the unlucky recipient of my mood swings. Hormones are a force of nature I couldn't tame.

At the ripe age of thirty-five, I was of "Advanced Maternal Age," a nice way of saying old. They used to call pregnancies like mine, "Geriatric". Thankfully, someone got wind that such phrasing was rude, and the medical terminology was updated. Because I was "advanced," my pregnancy was considered high risk. Being a little older when you're pregnant does come with a few perks—you receive additional tests to rule out chromosomal abnormalities, and you get extra, more frequent ultrasounds. Ultrasound appointments are always the most exciting appointments.

No one speaks in terms of weeks quite like a pregnant woman. Around week twenty-two, I went in for a standard glucose test. It's not uncommon for women to develop high levels of blood sugar while pregnant. By week twenty-three, I learned that I had developed gestational diabetes. This meant for the next seventeen weeks I would have to watch my diet and use a glucose monitoring test. I'm a wellness enthusiast and consider myself to be a healthy eater. But still, I had to reduce my carbohydrates and sugars. I had to forgo my beloved five bowls of cereal that I craved each day. In addition, I was required to prick my finger with a little needle to measure the glucose in my blood in the morning and after each meal. I would have made a lousy nurse; I'd often times screw up my first prick or two and have to keep trying until I drew a good blood sample. My finger pads were tender and blue.

Initially, the diagnosis scared me. My concerns for the baby were assuaged as my doctor reassured me the baby would continue to grow healthfully so long as I kept to the protocols. What I didn't expect to feel was some degree of shame around my diagnosis. I'm an Ayurvedic counselor; I teach people how to eat well and live a healthy lifestyle. Yet, here I am with diabetes. The shame was, of course, unfounded. I would never think poorly of a client who is dealing with an imbalance or an illness. I had to afford myself a similar level of compassion.

Pregnancy requires a woman to relinquish control. The saying babies are a miracle, has stuck for a reason. One day a woman is not pregnant, the next day she is! She carries on with her life. She answers emails, runs errands, and forgets to return texts… seasons change and her belly balloons. All the while, a person is forming inside her body; all without her doing. As a self-declared control freak, having so little control over such a large production was not easy. In a way, having gestational diabetes gave me some sense of control. I couldn't monitor my baby's heartbeat, the development of her organs, or the length of her little bones. But I could, and was advised to, prick my finger and catalog my blood sugar levels five times a day. Oddly, charting my little numbers, in my little notebook, felt soothing. It helped me feel like I was actively doing something.

As much as I say I hated pregnancy, I was, admittedly, one of those women who ambles around with their hand glued to their belly. The baby's impending arrival became more real the moment I felt my daughter's first kick. Her movements became my tangible evidence that things were progressing. Each movement indicated to me that she was thriving. My hand stayed attached to my belly while I worked, walked, and slept. By the third trimester, my short torso was full. Sitting was uncomfortable. Multiple times a day, for months on end, I walked around the lake in front of our house. I daydreamed. I wrote songs for my unborn baby, and hummed them in my head. A few times, while particularly lost in daydreams, I'd catch myself singing out loud. I still sing those same songs to Harper every night before bed. Oh geez, here I go getting all sappy. See this is what time will do; it sugar-coats memories—glossing them over like silky icing on a shabby cake. A page from my journal will give you a better sense of this reality:

Thirty-Three Weeks Pregnant

I barely slept last night. I keep getting tangled in my pregnancy pillow. By the time I get unleashed, I'm all wound up, and it's hard to fall back asleep. I'd stop using it, but my back hurts. Bad. I got called out yesterday. I asked my professor a question he apparently had just answered. It feels like the baby is somehow punching my bladder and simultaneously kicking my liver while I'm sitting in class. It's super distracting. I looked in the mirror this morning. My nipples are enormous. I haven't pooped in nearly a week. I'm going to take MiraLAX today.

There are, however, a few advantages to being pregnant; I didn't have to clean my hairbrush, or my shower drain for months. Thanks to the hormones that come during pregnancy, hair shedding ceased. We also get a break from buying tampons, and dealing with our periods. Especially towards the end, when walking is replaced by waddling, people are polite— holding doors, and offering their seats. Oddly, I had the libido of a college frat boy during my second and third trimesters. My husband was scared he'd "poke the baby," a concern I've read is more common than you might think... My elevated sex drive was shocking and undeniable. I bought my first vibrator. Nature is either funny, kind, or both. Nature knows a woman doesn't *feel* her sexiest while pregnant, so she serves us a hormonal cocktail that allows us to *experience* our sexiness. Nature is also wise to know that new moms are not going to have the energy or time to experience anything remotely erotic once the baby comes, so she throws us a bone ahead of time.

One of the most fascinating pieces of pregnancy is how it bonds women. Pregnant women find each other and ask, "How are you feeling?", "When are you due?"Elders offer advice, solicited or not, on what to expect, and what to do. While waddling around the lake, a lady pushing a Pomeranian in a stroller introduced herself as a pediatric nurse. I walked the same direction, passing her each morning. "You must be what, thirty-six weeks?" she asked. The next time I saw her, she said "You're carrying low, she's coming." Weeks later, she offered the advice, "Walk the other way"; by changing directions you'll induce labor." I laughed; people say the oddest things. I changed directions. There's an entire society of mothers—novice and veteran. Once someone is obviously pregnant, mothers come out of the woodwork to share their otherworldly experience of creating and caring for a tiny creature—an event, that for every mother, has left an indelible mark.

Pregnancy is time consuming. Especially towards the end. In the beginning, I went to the doctor once a month. Towards the end of my pregnancy, I went to the doctor once or twice a week. Visits were routine, and I learned the drill. Weight and blood pressure check upon arrival. Ultrasounds every-other visit. Once gestational diabetes was diagnosed, I became a star pupil—proudly handing the doctor my little notebook where I charted my glucose numbers.

I can recall a few standout doctor visits; especially one around the eleventh week, when the nurse took so many vials of blood for various tests that I nearly passed out. Extra nurses rushed over to place cold compresses on my head and draped me in warm blankets. I was humiliated. I thought, *"If I can barely handle getting blood drawn, how am I going to handle a human exiting my vagina?"* I was very nervous.

Week thirty-eight offered another little thrill. My fundal height was measuring small, so the doctor ordered an emergency ultrasound. The word 'emergency' before anything is not what a pregnant woman wants to hear. Luckily, it turned out that everything was fine. However, the baby was measuring small. During that appointment, my doctor informed me that the best practice would be to plan an induction for my fortieth week of pregnancy. At 10 PM, the night before my daughter's due date, I would be admitted to the hospital. Modern medicine would assist my daughter in arriving on her planned birthday. All I had to do now was...give birth.

CHAPTER 3

Birth Story

I wrote Harper's birth story in the form of a letter to her when she was just a couple of days old. At the time, I was flattened with both fatigue and joy; I was deep in the thick cocoon of being home with a newborn baby for the first time ever. In such, this account is rough and raw. I remember that I was crying while smiling as I wrote this letter. Now, as so much time has lapsed, I am glad I captured the event in real time, because there's no way my present-day recall would be accurate. I've chosen to keep Harper's birth-story in its unedited state—visceral and messy—just like childbirth.

Dear Harper,

You're here! Baby girl, the day you entered this world was the most significant and surreal day of my life. Daddy and I woke up on the day of our scheduled induction bursting with unparalleled anticipation. We were scheduled to be at the hospital at 10 PM, but mommy knew she'd be too anxious at home watching the clock all evening, so daddy and I went to our favorite cafe for dinner. Between you and my favorite meal, I went to the hospital with an extra full belly.

The hot summer night must have been an auspicious time for births. There were so many babies being born that night that we were admitted, but we could not get a birthing room. They were all full. Mommy got an IV and waited five hours in the triage area before finally starting the induction process (which is a pill that ripens mommy's cervix).

Daddy knew just what to do to help mommy stay calm as our vitals were being monitored and the clocked ticked in the corner of the room. I slipped in and out of slumber while daddy read mommy all the best jokes the internet could offer: "Why did the pregnant woman start shouting 'can't, won't, shouldn't, couldn't, don't'?" "Because she was having contractions." It's a grammar joke, get it? That's a glimpse into what you have to look forward to for at least the next eighteen years— horrendously delightful dad (and mom) jokes.

Around 3 AM, we were moved to our birthing room. It felt luxurious. Spacious and private— not like the traditional little hospital rooms with a shower drape dividing the beds like mommy imagined. Mommy received her cervix softening pill vaginally. The plan was to receive two of those over the course of eight to ten hours. Once the cervix was soft, mommy would then receive Pitocin, which is a medicine that would make mommy start to contract. From there, allegedly, you'd arrive anywhere between four to twenty-four hours later.

But you, my love, had other plans. Just three hours after I took my first cervix softening pill, my body started to contract on its own. It was a slow process. I never needed the Pitocin. It was your due date, and you were ready. I always appreciate punctual people—so thank you! Over the course of the next nine hours, my body cramped, contracted, and the dilation started. The pain was extreme, but I went twelve hours in labor before getting an epidural. In the interim, I had my first ever panic attack. I was anxious because your heart rate kept dropping. The nurses were active earth angels, guiding me to shift positions—from a yoga child's pose, to all fours, into supported hip openers with a big exercise balls between my legs. You and I are a clear match; even as you entered the world you created an excuse for mommy to do her yoga.

When the epidural kicked in, mommy's legs were useless. Limp and motionless. Your dad had to play an unexpectedly active role in the birthing process. Daddy helped the nurses move me into all these different positions. I had a catheter for my urine, a bare bum, and mascara smeared all over my face. It was my least glamorous moment. Labor is primal; there's zero space for inhibitions.

Then the bloody show came. That's what it's called. The name says it all. Daddy stepped up. He lifted bloody blanket pads and helped the nurses maneuver my limp body. The doctor expected this process to take hours and run late into the night, so daddy went to grab food from the hospital cafeteria. The doctor said she'd be back in a few hours. She shut the door behind her. Within minutes of the doctor's exit, your heartbeat fell dangerously low. The nurses quickly paged the doctor. Not thirty seconds later, the doctor was in the room, "It's go time. Let's push!" she said. I was fully dilated. As I started to push, your heartbeat plummeted. Daddy told me after the event, that he was extremely scared. I was exhausted. The doctor grabbed my hand, sternly looked me in the eyes, and with a tone that signaled this is life or death, she said, "Kristen, I need you to focus. It's time. I need you to push." I have chills as I write this. I knew it that second, the moment was critical. As the nurses grabbed my feet so I could bear down, another nurse paged for an emergency table in the OR (for an emergency c-section).

Physically, I did what the doctor said, mentally I was praying to God and talking to you. I felt with my whole being that I needed your spirit and the divine to make it through for you. With two or three prolonged contractions, I took a deep inhale, held my breath, tucked my chin to my chest, and pushed like hell. You were starting to come, but your heart-beat was alarmingly low. The situation was urgent; you needed to come out.

One of the nurses who took my vitals while I was being admitted recalled that I did yoga. "Aren't you a yogi? Can you grab your own feet, so you'll have better leverage?" she asked. "Of course!," I thought. I grabbed my feet and entered happy baby pose. Within five big pushes, you entered this world. Of course, you would choose to arrive through happy baby pose. You're such a cutie. If you had anything to do with the birth plan that became our reality—I must say, I appreciate your sense of humor.

When you arrived, the cord was wrapped around your neck. The doctor later told me that was likely the cause of your plummeting heartbeat. Thankfully, because of your strong spirit, the team of doctors and nurses that worked on us, daddy's love, and the angels that surround us, you arrived safely and full of vitality. Daddy said you came out silent and still, but when the doctor slapped you twice, you became alert. You whaled. I heard you scream, and daddy said to me, "Open your eyes". I looked down, and there you were, coming at me with a full head of hair, a gorgeously loud scream, followed by the most gratifying cry I've ever heard. I was flooded with relief. With gratitude. With the deepest love I've ever known. I held you, looked at daddy, and proceeded to cry ecstatically for the next twenty minutes.

Baby girl, we've loved you from the moment we saw a pink line on a Walgreens pregnancy test. Heck, I loved you even before that. But baby, the moment you entered the world, you became our whole world.

We love you.
Love,
Mom

CHAPTER 4

Sleep
(or Lack Thereof)

2:57 AM

Me: I haven't slept in 6 days. Can you please come over?
Mom: See you in the morning. I'll be there by 8.

That was the text I sent to my mom when my daughter was four days old. I consider myself to be a fiercely independent person, a trait it seems my daughter has inherited. After college, I moved to China to teach English. It was many years ago, well before the advent of Zoom and FaceTime, and I pretended that Skype didn't exist. I emailed regularly to check in, but I wanted to assert my independence and prove to myself that I could do things, even tricky things, alone.

I was pregnant during the era of Covid where your partner was not allowed to accompany you to doctor's visits, birthing mothers could only have one other person in the delivery room with them, and new parent's made their guests quarantine and test negative for the virus before meeting their newborn. A girlfriend of mine who had her son in the thick of Covid spoke so highly of the hidden blessing of not having any visitors during their son's first month of life. She, her husband, and baby bonded, and savored the quiet time to establish their connection as a unit of three. As a true introvert, the idea of a quiet, guest- free home appealed to me. My husband and I decided we would nest, just the three of us for at least two weeks. After a couple of weeks, we'd invite our parents and other guests to meet our little one. Nope, my daughter wasn't even a week old before I broke. *"Mom, I need you. Can you come stay with us for a few days?"* Unlikely words from an independent introvert, and yet, that's what I said because that's what I needed.

My brother and sister-and-law had a baby exactly one year to date before we did. It's sweet because the cousins share the same birthday. When I quizzed my brother and his wife on their experience as parents, they both reported that the lack of sleep was the biggest challenge. While pregnant, I asked every parent I met about their experience with a new baby. I listened as parents went on and on about the sleepless nights and unparalleled levels of fatigue. However, their stories went in one ear and out the other. I didn't get it.

By day three of being a mom, you guessed it. I got it. The fatigue is unfathomable. My eyes literally hurt from being open for too long. They stung. It wasn't the baby's fault. She slept great. In fact, newborns sleep a ton. You have to wake them to eat. My daughter was so snoozy, she would fall asleep while eating. A girlfriend wisely advised me to undress her before I feed her. "She'll feel a little cold, and that will keep her awake long enough to nurse before she falls to sleep again," she espoused.

Initially, the problem wasn't getting the baby to sleep—that problem came later. The challenge was getting ME to sleep. While I was in the hospital, we heard several calls of code blue come over the intercom. That is the emergency call used in medical settings to indicate a threat of life, alerting all hands to come on deck. The code blue calls inserted a level of anxiety within me that I couldn't seem to shake. Our hospital room, where we stayed for the forty-eight hours following Harper's birth, was decorated in bright orange flyers that said, "DON'T SLEEP HOLDING BABY. HOLDING BABY WHILE YOU'RE SLEEPING CAN CAUSE DEATH." Those flyers caught the attention of the anxious part of me and embedded a fear like no other into my psyche. Maybe that's where my postpartum anxiety began. Regardless of the cause, guess what else heightens anxiety? You guessed it—insomnia.

I suffered from insomnia for several months following the birth of my daughter. Harper slept as newborns do for the first few weeks—soundly. By week two, we discovered that she would only sleep if she was being held, or if she was snuggled in several blankets and warmly cradled in her sleep nest. The nurse in the hospital warned us that the babies should only sleep in a swaddle or in a sack, and should never be left unsupervised in a basinet, crib, or nest with blankets. "They can easily suffocate and die," I was told. I respected the warning, but medical language can be unnecessarily sharp and fear provoking. At Harper's two-week pediatrician appointment. I told the doctor that every time I put Harper in her bassinet to sleep, she cried uncontrollably, and that she would only sleep while bundled in blankets in a nest, or while being held. She indicated that is normal. Then she repeated what the hospital nurse advised: never fall asleep while holding her, and never leave her unsupervised in her nest with a blanket.

So, what did I do? What did my husband and I do, rather? For an entire month, we took turns guzzling coffee to stay awake while holding our sleeping baby, or watching her sleep in her nest directly next to us. Even at 2 AM, we forced ourselves awake, in shifts—scrolling on our phones, while our daughter rested peacefully. Our shift work, new parent, lifestyle was wreaking havoc on our wellbeing. We used our primary bedroom as the "sleeping room". That's where we took our shifts to be awake with the sleeping baby. We used our guest room as the "resting room," the place we went to sleep while the other parent watched the sleeping baby. It was insane. It was exhausting. But it's all we knew to do. Like I said, I entered motherhood profoundly clueless.

On occasion, my mom would drive across the state to hold and adore Harper while she slept, but even then, I was only able to sleep for short stints. By then, my husband had gone back to work. With someone else in the house to watch Harper sleep, in theory, I could have rested—but my attempts to doze usually failed. I entered the "resting room," crawled under my weighted blanket, turned on my *yoga nidra*—a guided sleep meditation, and slipped on my eye mask. I would exit the room and run downstairs to check on the baby an hour later. My anxiety ruined my ability to rest. I was reliably on edge. I couldn't take medication because I was nursing. And frankly, I was too sleep deprived to realize the gravity of the problem.

By month three, I was able to sleep well for three to four hours at a time. Then Harper would wake up, crying and hungry. I would nurse her and then fall back to sleep. I hadn't slept more than four hours in a row for months, but I was managing.

Month four is infamous for being the time of a "sleep regression". This is when the baby is making cognitive leaps in development that cause her sleep to be disrupted. Developmentally, it's a good thing. Practically—it is less so. Our month four sleep regression lasted sixty days. The regression persisted because I made lots of new mom mistakes. Harper would no longer sleep in a bassinet, so I let her take the bed, where for some reason she slept just fine. I knew I wasn't comfortable sleeping close to her in fear that I might unconsciously roll onto her, and I certainly didn't want her to roll off the bed. So, what did I do? I put my baby smack dab in the middle of our king-size bed, like a total queen, and I slept on the floor at the end of the bed. Meanwhile, my husband was relegated to sleeping exclusively in the "resting room" because his snoring would risk disturbing the baby and me. By the way, if you're laughing at the lunacy of this right now, don't worry—you're laughing with me; not at me.

This whole charade was still occurring when we went to visit my husband's family in the mountains of Colorado over Christmas. My sister-in-law had a one-and-a-half-year-old at the time. That baby slept like a saint, from 7 PM to 7 AM, with one three-hour nap in the middle of the day. Impressed, my head almost spun in circles like a cartoon character losing her mind when I learned of this sleep pattern. My sister-in-law is kind and was respectful enough to not judge my atrocious sleep habits. Nor did she give me unsolicited advice. But fortunately, I, had the wherewithal to observe her tactics, and take a few notes from her playbook. Thanks to her positive influence, by the end of the trip. Harper was sleeping, at least partially, in a crib; and I was off the floor and back in bed! By month seven, I was still holding Harper for all her naps, but she was sleeping through most of the night in her crib. By month ten, she was sleeping at night in her crib, and once a day in her crib. We were finally making progress.

Prior to motherhood, I assumed that babies came out of the womb tired and slept without hassle. Turns out, some babies do, and some babies don't. And for those who find sleep hygiene to be challenging, finally sorting out the life-consuming, sleep conundrum, feels like a marvelous accomplishment. For the first time since becoming a mom, I was sleeping at night, and had a couple hours a day for myself. I felt victorious! Although, still too revved up on hormones to *"sleep while the baby sleeps,"* meaning that I usually couldn't nap when I wanted to, I was at least able to rest.

Harper is now well over a year-old, and I not only sleep through the night like a normal human, but I also nap when she naps. With a toddler, nap time is sacred for mama. I look forward to noon on the weekends more than I'm proud to admit. Every weekend at noon I place Harper in her crib with her blanket and teddy bear, then I head straight to bed. I slide under my weighted blanket, put on my *yoga nidra*--sleep meditation, slip on an eye mask, and fall right into blessed, sacred, oh so missed, never again taken for granted, sleep.

P.S. Some times nap-time is tremendously disappointing—the baby refuses to sleep. On such occasions, I sulk into the nursery, pick up my daughter, and sit on the rocker to quietly read; small tears of dismay stream down my cheeks. New motherhood is sprinkled with moments of small wins, and small defeats. It's all okay.

CHAPTER 5

Baby Blues

Harper was just a few days old. My husband entered the room and saw that I was sobbing. I tried to talk through my weeping, "I'm so happy. I just can't stop crying. Don't worry. I'm really happy." My tear ducts had been highjacked. He looked worried; I looked pitiful. He wasn't buying it. "I have baby blues," I whimpered. I grabbed my phone to show him a screenshot from my Google findings. He'd believe Google. Come to find out, baby blues are an expected part of becoming a new mom. This happens because a cacophony of hormonal changes converges with the exhaustion of delivery, and novelty of having a tiny creature to care for—resulting in baby blues.

A few days after giving birth, the new mom commonly experiences wide fluctuations in her mood and has untamable crying spells. Why had I never heard of this? It baffles me that I attended nine months of doctor's appointments and spent days in the hospital—surrounded by well-informed nurses and doctors, and no one thought to give me a heads-up. There I was, initially, drenched in tears and needlessly confused as to why I felt this way. The baby blues came suddenly, and thankfully, left quickly. Within ten days, the blue drifted away. Of course, I was still navigating motherhood for the first time, so I continued to ride the full spectrum of human emotions, but at least the waterworks phase of motherhood had passed.

To be fair, I'm disappointed in my OB for not warning me that the baby blues are an expected part of the delivery and recovery process. Maybe the speed in which the blues came and went factored into why my doctors and nurses didn't bother to prepare me for such occurrences. Perhaps to people in the know, baby blues

are viewed as a short-term, standard, inconvenience—
to them, maybe they have bigger fish to fry. Personally,
I wish some women in the know would compile a list
of "normal" experiences to prevent new moms from
getting blindsided and feeling strange when such
events arise. My list would read as such:

1. During your second trimester, one's sex drive
    may reach new heights. Her partner will likely
    say things like, "Honey, what's gotten into
    you?" This is normal.

2. When the baby's umbilical cord falls off, a
    new mom may undergo big feelings over such
    a small event. She might have thoughts like,
    "Oh, no, my little girl is growing up so fast!
    Sooner than later, she'll be heading off to
    college." This is both absurd, as well as normal.

3. When a new mom goes to trim her baby's
    fingernails, she may fear that her daughter will
    twitch, or worse yet, she will flinch, resulting in
    harm. Because of this, a new mom might chicken
    out, and wait another day to attempt trimming
    her newborn's tiny nails. This is normal.

4. Four to ten days postpartum, a new mom may experience inconsolable crying spells. She will try her best, through the tears, to convince her partner she is happy. This is normal.

This list consists of off-the-cuff suggestions. Veteran mothers and medical professionals, please feel free to contribute to this list, as PSAs for new moms should be readily available. In brief, baby blues may not be avoidable, but being caught-off-guard by them is definitely preventable.

CHAPTER 6

Poor Timing

t's uniquely poor timing. A mother is literally handed the responsibility of taking care of an innocent, insatiably needy, sentient being, immediately following the most taxing event of her life—labor. I entered motherhood delirious and sore. Braxton Hicks contractions interrupted my sleep most nights throughout my third trimester. In the days leading up to my daughter's induction, I was jolted awake several times a night. I Googled to learn this alarming sensation is called "lightening crotch." Each time I woke up, I remembered the reason I was experiencing electric pressure was because my baby was just days away. A blend of discomfort and excitement completely hindered rest.

My doctor scheduled my induction for the night before Harper's due date. I brought my favorite pillow and sleep mask from home. I naively expected to check in, receive the pill that would start to soften my cervix, and be able to drift to sleep. I'd wake up with the sun to start the birthing process. What a joke. Within hours, I was hooked to tubes and monitors. I was up. The pain started soon after. And it lasted another seventeen hours.

I had already been awake for nearly forty-eight hours straight when Harper arrived. It was hands down the best moment of my entire life. I was super jacked-up on adrenaline and love. There's no way I could sleep then. Within hours, a nurse walked me through a brief tutorial on how to breastfeed. Harper latched right away. She came out hungry. A lactation consultant came the next morning. She taught me various positions: the cradle, the cross-cradle, and the side-lying position. Unbeknownst to me, I would come to know these positions well for the subsequent fourteen months. Breastfeeding would be a huge part of my duty. That night, delirious and sore, my work began.

We had to stay in the hospital for several extra nights because the doctors needed to make sure my gestational diabetes wasn't passed on to Harper. My husband was given a hospital bed to match mine directly next to me. There we were, two sleep deprived, clueless, new parents, and one tiny little human. For the next two days and nights, I nursed. We took turns holding the baby, changing diapers, and watching her sleep. During our final hours at the hospital, we found out there was something called a "night nursery," where the newborns can go to be taken care of by nurses while the parents sleep. That would have been nice to know sooner.

I left the hospital equipped with postpartum wound care. Every hour, on the hour, I had to tend to my wounds. I wore massive maxi pads lined with cooling, which-hazel pads inside of an adult diaper. I cleaned my episiotomy stitches with cold water, and sprayed my vagina with anti-itch spray that was sent straight from the havens. I quickly ordered a twelve pack online. My belly felt deflated and achy. My milk was coming in, and my boobs were gigantic and rock hard. Initially, I was nervous about having to pee. I worried the urine would burn. I was even more terrified to poop. What if I tore my stitches? The nurses cautioned me that this was a common concern. They gave me stool softeners, and told me to relax. Once home, every so often I'd go to the bathroom and a blood clot the size of a golf ball would fall into the toilet. A few days in, I got up the courage to use a mirror and examine the scene. I expected horror. Battle wounds. Nope, just a row of little stitches—all healed up. The human body is incredible.

I don't share any of these details to be graphic. This is just the type of stuff that caught me by surprise. Sure, the baby is precious, but the aftermath of birth isn't pretty, so we as a culture tend to skip these details. In all those months of being pregnant, in all the advice I received, not a single person mentioned how common it is to fear a bowel movement after giving birth. No one illustrated for me how painfully tired a new mom promises to be. Not a single person shared with me how they returned home from the hospital hopped up on adrenaline and at the same time, clouded with fatigue. I expected my daughter to come home from the hospital in a diaper. I had no idea that I'd be wearing one too.

CHAPTER 7

Division of Labor

Well-known author, Anne Lamott, wrote, "Expectations are resentments under construction." Prior to my daughter's arrival, my husband and I spent hours theorizing how we'd care for our new baby. He'd take two weeks off for paternity leave. *"The baby will be mostly sleeping, and I'm the only one who can feed her, so you can go to the gym. Focus on your health and please pick up my groceries,"* I naively advised him.

Nearly two years before becoming a mother I decided to go back to school to earn my Master's Degree in Psychology and Clinical Mental Health Counseling. Luckily, I was able to complete my course work before the baby arrived. I emailed my professor my final submissions just hours before heading to the hospital. My plan was to take ninety days off, to focus on motherhood, before wrapping up my internship. I needed to earn 1,000 hours of clinical work before being able to graduate. I told my yoga and Ayurveda clients I'd be on maternity leave for three months as well.

In the months leading up to maternity leave, I felt excited. I was optimistic that caring for a newborn would feel like a break, in contrast to seeing clients, attending classes, and completing graduate assignments while pregnant. I expected to wear comfy clothes, nurse, stare adoringly at my baby, nap when she napped, and take long walks with the stroller. I expected, without communicating, for my husband to give the baby baths, hold her when I needed to do tasks that required both hands, and continue to engage with me like we always had—like a couple.

I was unaware that my baby would only sleep while being held. I didn't know that she wouldn't like the stroller and I'd need to carry her everywhere. I was ignorant of her preference to nap mostly while being worn and walked. She was a baby shark. If I stopped moving, she woke up. I totally forgot that I needed time to continue coloring my hair, do our laundry, and put the dishes away. I didn't account for all the stuff I'd need to research and buy. We'd been generously gifted and received mounds of baby supplies at my shower. I thought I was set. I was completely oblivious to the tasks of pumping to maintain supply, and the added task of cleaning all the pumping equipment. It never crossed my mind that someone would need to change the diaper pales, and sanitize every surface after major blowouts. I forgot about all the pediatric appointments, and my inability to get a haircut or go to the dentist. Because who will hold or wear my baby shark and walk around with her while I was getting worked on?

My expectations were not based on the reality that was to come. And my expectations screwed me. I was exhausted. I was resentful. *"I feel like I'm doing everything,"* I told my husband. That of course was an unfair, one-sided perspective. In truth, my resentment had nothing to do with my husband. He offered to help, and did his best. It wasn't his fault he couldn't give birth, produce breastmilk, or soothe the baby by the sheer smell of his pheromones.

I quickly learned about *"the fourth trimester"*, the three-month period after the baby is born. Energetically, the baby is still an extension of her mother. The physical and emotional bond is immutable. During that period, if our daughter was crying, there was little to nothing my husband could do to soothe her. He would change her diaper and cuddle her, but more often than not, she whaled until she was back in my arms. During that period, I experienced fantom kicks. I would feel throbs in my abdomen like she was still in there. I would hear fantom cries; the sound of her helpless voice screaming, even when she was silent. The connection was intense and disorienting.

Being a mother occupied all my time and consumed more energy than I had. I was underprepared for the nonstop demands of motherhood. I was overwhelmed.

And I undeservingly blamed my husband. As Father's Day approached, I felt myself getting more and more pissed off. I bought my husband a card and gift, but I was filled with anger. *"Why on earth do we celebrate fathers when mothers are the ones who do all the work?"* I thought. I caught myself entertaining such cold, and bitter thoughts. I did my best to therapized myself. The night before Father's Day I made a list of all the reasons I appreciate my husband. I itemized all the ways he supports me. I reframed my belief that I was the one doing all the work. I reminded myself that biology and culture are not systems of equality, and that we were both doing our best. I reminded myself we were a team. We went to the aquarium of Father's Day. A 700-pound, majestic dolphin starred at Harper through aquarium glass, and she giggled at toddlers with balloons. We took touristy family photos in front of a green screen. We bought them because we wanted to remember the wonderful day.

The division of labor became more balanced as time passed. Around the six-month mark I felt an ostensible shift. Brian started giving Harper her evening baths. I would catch them reading books and singing songs. I witnessed Father/Daughter bonding before my eyes. *"Dance to the beat. Harper move your feet. Boop Boop Boop"*, Brian would sing, and Harper would bounce and giggle in his lap. I felt my shoulders relax and drop. My lips and eyebrows softened from their pinched expression. The topic of resentment isn't a popular one. It never feels good to think poorly, let alone speak poorly, of your partner. It's borderline embarrassing and shameful to admit any of this. But it's also honest. And there's something therapeutic about truth. It sets us free from this false notion that partnership, let alone partnership while parenting is easy. Because it is not.

Harper: two months old

I remember a time when I would have said, "just a stay-at-home mom" or "just takes care of a baby". I didn't know then what I know now—"just" includes:

24-7:
attentiveness
problem solving
planning and
imperfect patience

24-7:
caring
service and
affection
Inside 'just' lives being okay with being:
messy
tired
late and
knowing things are going to be a little undone

While also 'just':
constantly thinking about someone other than self
All while 'just' trying to maintain:
friendships
intimacy
patience and
some semblance of identity beyond motherhood
So yea, I didn't get it. There is no 'just' in being a
mom. Whether one is at home all day, returning
to an outside career, or somewhere in between—
being a mom is anything but 'just'.
Moms, I get it now.

CHAPTER 8

Relationships

There's a loneliness that comes with having a newborn baby. Taking care of an infant requires one to keep weird hours. I was often awake at 2 AM when the rest of the world was sleeping. I felt disconnected from the old me, and my old life. My husband and I were having two different experiences as parents. The elders in my life wore rose-colored glasses. They had long forgotten the delirium of being a first-time mom. My friends texted me and dropped by for the occasional visit. I enjoyed their presence, yet in their company, I often found myself faking sanity, and trying not to gush about the baby, or vent about the state of overwhelm I was in.

In the beginning, too, there were the components of anxiety and insomnia that kept me isolated. I found myself reconnecting with distant friends from much earlier seasons of life. We'd send each other book recommendations, and links to our favorite podcast episodes. Those loose connections made via text and social media that didn't require much energy were all I had the bandwidth to handle at the time. Although, too much social media only exacerbated the loneliness.

Humans are social creatures, so I tried to get out. I'd often devise a game plan to leave the house. I'd pep talk myself into a trip to Target or a walk with a girlfriend on the other side of town. These plans often resulted in lots of false starts. I'd finally get the baby in the car, all strapped in and ready to go, but then she'd need to eat, or poop, or sleep. I was running on fumes, and felt easily defeated. As a result, I stayed home a lot. An introvert by nature, I didn't miss large social gatherings. But I did miss witty banter, as well as deep conversations. However, I simply didn't have the cognitive readiness for either.

I caught myself in moments of envy over my friends who hadn't yet had kids. I was jealous of their freedom. They could take a shower and blow-dry their hair anytime. Like anytime. How had I taken that luxury for granted for so many years? I had a new respect for friends who had chosen not to procreate. That came with it's obvious advantages too. I developed a deeper sympathy for friends struggling with infertility. Being a new mother gave me an enriched level of understanding for my clients with children, and great admiration for how they took time in the midst of motherhood to take care of themselves. In time, I found my way. Best friends shifted into the role of "Aunties," and I started making new friends. Harper had a passionate distaste for the carseat. Proximity became a deciding factor in how often I'd see people. I found myself gravitating towards people who had kids, and who forgave my tardiness due to a mistimed feeding. There was an organic kinship with people who completely understood how one could lose their train of thought mid-sentence.

Partnerships are complex. And in a couple, when two become three there is an adjustment period. It took about a year for Brian and me to find our equilibrium. We now have scheduled date nights, where we get to undress from our roles as mom and dad and hang out as a couple. We order wine and appetizers, and invariably end up talking about Harper at some point.

My favorite development occurred between my own mother and me. I started seeing my mom differently nearly the moment I became pregnant. I thought, *"If my mom loved me even a fraction of the amount, I already love my baby, that's a lot of love."* My mind was blown by the capacity for a person to love another person. Once I had a newborn, I grew more appreciative towards my mom because (A) she offered to help and was Harper's baby whisperer. She could soothe her on demand. And (B) because I had come to realize how demanding babies are. I was a baby once. Undoubtedly, I was needy. And my mom took care of me. It's been fun to see my mom as a grandmother. I've watched her with my niece and nephews over the years. She's softened. She no longer cares about protecting the white sofas or keeping the fridge free of fingerprints. I take pleasure in seeing her drop into this incredibly playful version of herself with my own daughter. Virtually all my relationships changed when I became a mother. One of my brothers had kids a decade before me. My other brother had a kid just one year before me. So now we find ourselves chatting about salacious topics like how Costco ran out of diapers.

CHAPTER 9

Travel

rian and I took our first trip when Harper was
about six weeks old. I use the word *trip* loosely
because we were just visiting my mom at her beach
house, about 100 miles away. The journey should have
taken about three hours, but it somehow took over
eight. We kept having to stop for Harper to nurse,
then burp, then change diapers, then nurse again—
nope not hungry; try again in an hour. We were on
and off the highway a dozen times. Five hours into the

trip, I suggested that we stop for the night and book a hotel. My husband and I had to laugh at the lunacy.

We brought so much baby gear that Brain could barely see out of the rearview mirror. We had our usual luggage, a bouncer, a collapsible bathtub, a lifetime supplies of diapers, and tents to block the sunshine. The amount of stuff was only made more ridiculous by the fact that my mom had already equipped the beach house with a bassinet for this visit, as well as a highchair and swing for future use. I've heard, the saying that goes "the smaller the baby, the bigger the gear." It's so true. The trip was, of course, worthwhile. It was a joy to see my siblings hold and adore my baby. It was adorable to see my little niece and nephews view Harper like she was an exotic species in an aquarium—too fragile to touch, but semi-interesting to look at.

That winter, we traveled to Colorado to see my husband's family for Christmas. The trip coincided with the period in Harper's life where she would only nap while being held and walked. It was easy to fulfill those conditions when we were home in Florida; it was seventy degrees and sunny—I just strapped her to me, and lapped around the lake a dozen times a day. But in Colorado, things were completely different. It was twelve degrees in Colorado, which was certainly not conducive for napping outside. I ended up wearing Harper while walking around in the bedroom and going up and down the indoor hallways. I read books while I paced around. Maybe it was the altitude, or lack of sleep; but in my entire life, I've never stubbed my toe or ran into doorframes more often.

When Harper was one year old, we made another trip to Colorado. We were going to spend a week at an Airbnb in the mountains, then stay a week with my in-laws. I was so excited to go. I told a client I would be away for two weeks because I was going on vacation. He said, *"My wife and I referred to traveling with our kids as trips, not vacations. Traveling with a baby is never a vacation."* He wasn't trying to be a downer. I got the sense he and his wife have laughed about the truism over the years. Turns out, he was right. By the time we got to my in-laws, I was wiped! Harper was at a stage where she could crawl faster than I could walk; she was investigative and got into everything. I thought I had prepared for the trip by packing plastic safety plugs for outlets, and plastic latches for cabinets. Unfortunately, the Airbnb had outdated electrical sockets, and my safety plugs kept falling out. Harper was crafty and she soon figured out how to move the barricade of chairs and suitcases I built to block the steep staircase. I filled every waking hour possible with activities outside the rental. When we were there, I was endlessly pulling her away from outlets and chasing her up the stairs. I learned that it's very tricky to baby-proof a home away from home. Once again though, the trip was worth it. My in-laws became incandescent in the presence of their granddaughter, and I was smiling ear to ear watching Harper play with her older cousin, and gently "pet" her baby cousin.

From an early age, I've been intoxicated by the lure of far-away places, and culture different from my own. Traveling is in my DNA. Historically, long flights haven't bothered me; I would always get lost in books, then curl up like a cat and snooze until touchdown. Traveling with a baby in her first year of life, however, is immensely different. Varied environments, time zones, and altered schedules add another layer to an already capricious time. But since then, we've been on several trips, and traveling with a baby has gradually become easier. As the baby gets bigger, the amount of necessary gear does shrink. We're no longer lugging around collapsible bathtubs and highchairs. One fine day, we'll retire the diaper bag; Harper will carry her own passport, and we'll go on a real *vacation*.

Harper: four months old

My baby doesn't care how much I weigh.

She has no preference over a messy-dirty bun, or clean blowout.

She thinks nothing of my accolades.

She isn't concerned about my finances or if I've responded to all my emails.

My baby values me for one reason…

I love.

Maybe we have a lot to learn from babies.

CHAPTER 10

Daycare

I expected there would be more tears. From her, yes, but more-so from me. When I dropped my little girl off at daycare for the first time, neither of us cried. In fact, the moment I placed Harper in Miss Mays' arms, she grinned. I gave her a quick kiss good-bye, and that was it. I expected to feel pangs of mom-guilt, but instead, I pressed "play" on my podcast app and drove away feeling a wave of relief. The decision to put Harper in daycare didn't come easily for me. On one hand, I wanted to be spend as much time as possible with my baby girl. But on the other hand, I found myself frequently restless, bored, and tired. I was craving variety and alone-time. I've longed believed daycare to be a healthy option for families. I was a daycare kid myself. My baby-book is plastered with images of me in fluffy dresses—coloring, playing with kitchen sets, and being ostensibly doted on by teachers. But was daycare right our family? I went back and forth on this issue hundreds of times.

Once I finally decided to enroll Harper in daycare, I was met with great disappointment. I eagerly made calls to every daycare and learning center within a fifteen-mile radius. And I was informed that every facility had waitlists. One school even said, "She'll be in kindergarten before a spot opens here. There are sixty families ahead of you." I wish someone would have told me that if one is remotely considering daycare, call ahead, while you're still pregnant, because there's a good chance that unbelievably long waitlist awaits. We were placed on a waitlist for eight long months before we finally got in.

In the weeks leading up to Harper's first day, I told my husband that I was truly considering psych-meds, a slew of herbal remedies, or daily visits with a therapist. Being the primary caretaker of our little girl had taken a toll on me. I was physically and emotionally depleted. My tank was recognizably empty. I was overdue for a change in our family operations. I had reached the point where I felt that I could no longer be in the role of a hands-on mother most of the time. The timing, as the universe would have it, was perfect. A spot finally opened up, and we were able to get Harper in. Harper is happy in daycare. I drop her off each morning; she eats her breakfast at a miniature table with four of her closest friends. They feast on Cheerios and thin slices of pear. When I pick her up in the afternoon, I am greeted with the most enthusiastic hug. She normally wears a big smile, as well as the remnants of finger-paint from arts and crafts. Daycare has been an absolute godsend for us. Harper thrives in the company of her peers, and daycare has afforded me space to re-connect with the parts of me that exist outside of mothering.

Harper: thirteen months old

When I am with my baby 24-7, for night-feeds, breakfasts, and the repeated events that fill days, and spill into new seasons—I daydream about a life with some space between me, my baby, and the repetitive nature of caretaking. I find myself walking around the lake in the afternoon. Harper is in her stroller; two fans are blasting hot, wet air into her face while she reads her farm animal book. It's upside down. She licks the pages; enjoying the way the sheep's fur feels on her tongue. We've done the same walk hundreds of times this year. My mind wanders to visions of an alternate version of reality where I get to peruse books in The British Library. I daydream about a girl's trip to tropical locations; saliva puddles as I can almost taste the mint from my imaginary mojito. I envision myself in "real clothes"; slim-fit trousers, and kitten heals. I'm currently wearing spandex shorts, and a tank with a built-in bra. The elastic that has been stretched out. My mind paints a reality so far from the one I'm living. This is where my mind goes when it wanders. But as alluring as it all sounds, this is absolutely not where my heart lives. My heart lives with my daughter; with the grin and giggle that spontaneously burst from her tiny body; with the way she says "Mama," and how she claps when she wakes up in the morning. We're on day five of daycare. It's only noon and I'm writing because I have to actively busy myself, so don't rush to pick her up, and disrupt a room full of napping one-year olds. I miss her. I will pick her up soon. We'll nurse, sing songs on the way home, play, eat again, and by the time we go on our afternoon stroll there's a good chance I'll be daydreaming again. This is the paradox of motherhood. I want to be constantly near her, and when near for long enough, I dream of space.

CHAPTER 11

Breastfeeding

It had been fourteen months, and I was finally weaning. My boobs were engorged, rock-hard, and incredibly painful. I stuffed frozen cabbage leaves in my bra; twenty minutes later, I smelled like old salad—wilted cabbage leaves cupped my breasts as I returned to the freezer for replacements. In my experience, there are three stages to the breastfeeding: contemplation, latch and release:

STAGE 1: Contemplation...Will I be able to breastfeed, and do I want to?

Within this phase, I was bombarded with well-meaning advice, cultural pressure, and fear. *Do I want to host a tea party for one on my chest a dozen times a day? What if I can't produce? What if she doesn't latch? What if my milk turns on like a faucet and it soaks through all my shirts?* Once I decided that I wanted to try to breastfeed, the rest of the questions were out of my hands. I bought a couple of nursing bras, a pack of nipple pads, and left the rest up to the universe. Harper came out ready for milk. Brian jokes about her super-human strength. We have a recording on his phone of this seven-pound creature performing an upward scoot, and a pushup, in pursuit of my nipple within seconds of being born. Harper latched quickly. My milk came in. I had a few dips where I reached to various lactation supporting supplements and teas, to make sure my milk kept coming, but basically, I got lucky, and it was a non-issue.

STAGE 2: Latch

The connection between mother and baby is unparalleled, and it is made even more intense by the rush of oxytocin that floods a mother's body as a result of a baby's suckling. Nature certainly was savvy to manufacture this sweet chemical cocktail. It bonds us, making us happier, and more generous when it comes to sharing all our food and energy. In hindsight, I want to say I loved every moment of nursing. It was always sweet and intimate. But that's not true. Sometimes I hated it. *Why was this so time-consuming?* (Newborns can take forty-five minutes per session, and they eat every two hours. You do the math). Harper wouldn't take a bottle, so that meant her meals were 100% on me. Literally. Around four months, when she was becoming aware of her environment, she became easily distracted while nursing. To help maintain her focus, I resorted to feeding her alone, while in dark rooms. Most of the time, nursing felt like the most precious experience of my life, but there were also occasions where it felt like an isolating chore, that I so desperately wanted to outsource. As Harper became more mobile, her approach to nursing morphed from passive to acrobatic. She took an interest in crawling all over me, and latching from inverted positions. She practiced her downward facing dog, and half-moon yoga poses, all while drinking her milk. Quiet moments for nourishment transitioned into moments that served more for play and comfort than for food. At this point, it was time for stage three.

STAGE 3: Release.

Weaning was a bittersweet experience for me. On one hand, I was anxious to have my body back for me again. Between pregnancy and nursing, my body had existed as a growing tank and feeding station for twenty-six months. For the better part of two years, I felt like my body belonged more to Harper than to me. I was excited about the prospect of balancing my hormones, getting my libido back, and finally, being able to use Botox again. On the other hand, Brian and I had no plans to get pregnant again anytime soon, which meant nursing was likely a once-in-a-lifetime experience for me. As Harper neared her first birthday, I was leaning towards weaning, but she wasn't ready. Around month fourteen, Harper just lost interest.

Rather than encouraging her to continue, I leaped on the opportunity to stop nursing.

This sounds wild, but I had a lot of fear around how stopping breastfeeding would affect the bond Harper and I shared. *Would she still need me if I wasn't nursing her? Would we still feel close?* These questions sound ludicrous, but my entire experience of being a mom involved breastfeeding my baby. Nursing felt like a huge part of our relationship, and an identifier in my role as a mom. Obviously, a mom is no less a mom if she nourishes her baby with a bottle or food. Throughout the weaning process, Harper replaced nursing with cuddling. She stayed close and proved that my concerns were unnecessary.

Physically, by the time Harper decided she wanted to wean, my body had already reduced production. However, the adjustment was still excruciating. To alleviate the throbbing discomfort, I alternated between ice packs and frozen cabbage leaves that I cupped around my bumpy, veiny, engorged breasts. Our weaning process took about a week. Once complete, I booked my Botox appointment, and re-hung all my high-necked shirts and dresses that were impractical to wear when I was nursing. A week later, my boobs returned to normal, and I felt so free! I was blissfully unaware of the impending hormonal avalanche that would ensue in the coming weeks. I thought I'd feel amazing after I stopped nursing. I did not. My hormones didn't undergo another wave of adjustments—they underwent a tsunami. I experienced undulating surges of grief, irritability, and even rage. Within four to six weeks, I felt regulated, and the process of weaning on all levels was behind me. Thank goodness!

Poop

Had I not been warned, I would have been very concerned at the sight of Harper's first bowel movement. I read that a baby's first poop resembles tar—dark and sticky. I felt like a pro, as I used a warm washcloth to remove the tree-like resin that was securely adhered to Harper's tiny booty. Babies create a vast array of bowel movements in the first few months. We went through a long period of these seedy, turmeric-colored stools that no diaper could seem to contain. During that period, blow-outs were a common occurrence. A blow-out is exactly as it sounds; an inordinate amount of poop somehow ejects out of the tiny baby, obliterating the confines of her diaper. A remarkable amount of excrement smears up the baby's back, and all surrounding fabrics are destroyed. It's a scene.

Harper's colon had a sense of humor. These blow-outs were uniquely timed to occur in her carseat, or when she was in public. One epic blow-out took place when Harper was about three months old and we were nearing the end of one of the120-mile road trips we took to visit my family. Upon arrival, Brian and I did our best to clean the seat, but it was impossible to remove the lingering smell. Hours later, while traveling home, Harper was so upset that she started to vomit. The only way I could soothe her was to drape a blanket over her carseat to block the light and stimulation. I then proceeded to duck my head under the blanket to gently rub her head while repeating, "Shhh shhh shh", as a mother does. I essentially hotboxed myself into an "aromatic" confined space of bodily fluids. Finally, she fell asleep, and I was able to come out, and up for some fresh air.

Poop stories are commonplace for new moms. I practice Ayurveda, which is a holistic form of medicine. The modality focuses on gut health and uses observation and self-report of one's bowel movements as a diagnostic tool. Talking about poop, is for me, shop talk. Oddly, the poop of an infant doesn't really smell. Or at least, it didn't in my experience. That all changed once we introduced solid foods. There's no need to go into detail, but let's just say, by that point, I was very grateful for the odor trapping technology of our Diaper Genie.

Throughout pregnancy, and new motherhood, my colon was on a misadventure as well—mainly by way of constipation. Infrequent, dry, pellet-like stools are common for pregnant women. My husband was kind enough to buy Costco size bags of prunes. Unfortunately, they didn't help. I employed all of my Ayurvedic tricks: I ate mostly warm, moist foods, I drank hot water, I added ghee to hot water in the morning, and massaged my belly with warm sesame oil—which helped to prevent stretch marks. My bowels may have been even worse without these measures, but still, I was not regular. As my belly expanded, I grew to rely heavily on Metamucil and MiraLax. By the time Harper was around nine months old, both our systems had adjusted, and our plumbing issues were finally cleared up. How's that for shop talk?

CHAPTER 13

Baby Brain

Harper: seven months old

Why did I think baby brain was an anomaly that occurred only during pregnancy? I'm constantly searching for words. Very ordinary words. Yesterday I could not for the life of me recall the word, turquoise. I know I'm not dumb, but I've been feeling dumb lately. I feel like I've forgotten how to talk to adults. I answered my phone in a sing-song voice today. It was a new client. I sounded like I was a guest star on The Muppets— so embarrassing. She booked a session, but I won't be shocked if she thinks more deeply about my tone, and decides to cancel. I'm not used to feeling so incompetent. I probably need to write "I am smart. I am smart. I am smart" on sticky notes. Affirmations (and a list of commonly used words) would probably serve me well right now. I hope baby brain isn't a life-long impediment.

CHAPTER 14

food

Sleep, poop, and food; these are the three pillars of any woman's pregnancy and early motherhood journey. Foundational for life and happiness, we must discuss food. We'll begin with pregnancy. We've all heard about pregnant women having bizarre cravings for foods such as pickles and ice cream. My mom craved kiwis; it was the 80's—before everything was global and in season somewhere. They were hard to find and pricey. My mom tells stories about sending my dad all over town on procurement missions. My cravings didn't kick in until the second trimester. Food aversions dominated my life during the first twelve to sixteen weeks of my pregnancy. The smell of nearly everything made me sick. My husband could barely heat up a bowl of soup without me wanting to yak. I ate mostly cereals, crackers, and cold sandwiches. By the sixteenth week of pregnancy, I was texting my husband with urgent requests for watermelon and pears. I was nostalgic for foods of my childhood. I hadn't had Wendy's chili or A-1 steak sauce in well over twenty years, but all of a sudden, I had unstoppable cravings for those things. I'd been a vegetarian for fifteen years, but I longed for the taste of chicken throughout my pregnancy. I thought it was important to trust and honor my body, so I suspended that ideology. Also, once I found out I had gestational diabetes, I needed to adjust my diet, and eating a variety of protein just made sense for me. By week thirty, my torso was out of room, and I felt chronically full. At that point, my cravings dissipated, and I enjoyed more frequent small meals.

Caring for a newborn and cooking for myself felt incompatible. I ordered catered meals from my favorite restaurant. Trays of roasted sweet potato, grilled broccoli, spiced rice, and sesame tofu kept me satisfied for weeks. As Harper grew, I realized how calorically expensive breastfeeding can be. I easily became faint if I didn't eat every few hours. I also noticed that I had to hydrate a lot to keep my milk supply up. I found myself physically depleted around months seven through nine. Harper was just starting to eat purees and solids, but most of her nourishment was still coming from me. She was drinking more milk than ever, and looking back, I could have used more food myself to keep up with those demands. By the time Harper was eleven or twelve months, she was proficient with her table foods, and my body only needed to provide supplemental nutrition and comfort feeds. By the one-year mark, I was able to return to my pre-baby nutritional practices, with one caveat—taking care of a toddler can be an athletic pursuit. To keep up my energy, I treat myself to snack times with Harper. Prior to becoming a mom. I really wasn't a snack food person, but I've grown fond of teddy grahams and goldfish with my little girl.

Now let's talk about baby food. What a mess! We first introduced Harper to "real food," around month six or seven. Out of the gate, she was more interested in feeling the texture of mushed bananas and sliced avocado between her fingers, than actually eating anything. We spent twenty minutes with her in the highchair, exploring colors, textures, and injecting only minuscule amounts of food into her mouth. Then I spent another twenty minutes cleaning up the mess. Her ability to splatter pureed prunes onto surfaces across the room was impressive. My camera reel is filled with images of her chubby cheeks painted in orange sweet potato, and red tomato sauce. At one of her appointments, the pediatrician asked if she was eating solids. I reported, "I serve them three times a day; collective, she probably consumes about a tablespoon a day"."Great", the pediatrician exclaimed. "It's all about introducing textures, and tastes. It's okay if she's not eating much yet. I know it's a lot of effort for a bite or two, but it's important," she explained.

We carried on. By month ten, we couldn't leave for a walk without a container full of Cheerios. When she finished her container, that was my cue to head home. In no time, she was devouring full cups of Mac n' cheese, and yellow rice. Food is such a simple pleasure, and there's something about watching a baby enjoy food that's uniquely satisfying. As Harper continues to grow, her need for nourishment feels incessant. If I'm not offering food, she's asking for it. She often takes two bites and then wanders away. We repeat the cycle twenty times a day. I joke that being a mom has turned me into an Italian Grandmother; I'm constantly offering food. It's sweet, though. For most meals, we eat together. I dish up her food before squeezing an inordinate amount of Sriracha onto my meal. Invariably, she borrows from my plate, takes one spicy bite, grabs her little tongue says, "Hot hot." she gulps water from her sippy cup, and then returns for more. One day, soon enough, we'll go for sushi, and I'll teach her all about wasabi.

CHAPTER 15

Mom—Rage

The bottom platform of our staircase is large and angular; no normal baby gate could effectively block the opening. I configured an adjustable fence, normally used to create a playpen, to block off the stairs. One afternoon, for the fifth time that day, Harper evaded the makeshift gate and was climbing up the stairs. As per usual, my heart sank, my body flooded with adrenaline, and I rushed to catch and rescue her. (She hadn't learned how to safely use the steps yet). Once safely in my arms, I let out this primal, animalistic grunt. It was so loud. I sounded like a hippopotamus in labor. The sound confused Harper and scared the shit out of me. I was fuming.

A few weeks after I stopped nursing, I started to experience anger on a whole new level. I can, admittedly, become irritable and impatient; but I've never been an angry person. The feeling of anger had me not only mad, but also scared. I would never hurt my daughter—that's for sure. I wasn't frightened I'd lose my temper and physically react under any circumstance, but I was worried that my charged energy would negatively impact my daughter emotionally. I did my best to take deep breaths and recite mantras, "Breathe." "You're a good mom having a hard time." "She's not giving you a hard time; she's having a hard time." Breath and mantras provided some relief, but I still found myself on the edge of being irate several times a day, for several weeks. I couldn't pinpoint exactly where the anger was coming from. It arrived out of the blue. Harper was about fourteen months old. She was developing a sense of independence. She was mobile and was starting to develop strong preferences. She didn't have much of a vocabulary at that point, so she was starting to express her big feelings through sounds and mini tantrums. Sure, no one likes to be around a flailing, screaming child, but my feelings did not match my reality. Even in my anger, I understood she was just a young toddler, behaving like a young toddler.

I considered how much of an effect my hormones were having on my moods. I knew that weaning would be challenging on the physical level; my breasts would engorge, and there would be some discomfort as my milk dried up; but I was not expecting the cessation of nursing to have such a large effect on my hormones and temperament. During this period of rage, I found myself engulfed with shame. How could a mother who loves her child more than anything in the world, a woman who practices yoga and meditation, and presents herself as being so peaceful, be filled with anger? I assumed that it would take some time for my hormones to level out, but I wanted to be proactive. I could not continue to harbor such heated emotions. So, I started taking a few supplements to promote calmness, and I searched for resources. I stumbled upon a podcast on "mom-rage". I knew instantly that's what I was experiencing. The podcast featured a child psychologist. The golden takeaway for me was that mom-rage is the result of a mother's unmet needs. Yes, unmet needs. This resonated deeply.

I had been working part-time, completing my grad-school internship, and staying home with a baby for over a year. A confluence of events had just occurred; Harper started daycare, weeks later she started weaning, and weeks later I began to experience bouts of anger. With Harper in daycare, I was working more, and filling my "free time" with writing. I could feel intuitively and in my bones that was I needed was rest. I needed downtime to rejuvenate; but because, although I would never judge another mom for putting her kid and daycare, and I know it was the best decision for our family— I was feeling guilty for putting Harper in daycare. Thus, I wasn't allowing myself to rest. With that realization, I resolved in that moment, to allow myself to curl up with a book, watch a movie, or nap as often as I needed.

The next day I took the additional step of booking a session with a therapist. Like I said, I feared my own anger. I was motivated to pursue as many outlets as necessary to dismantle the charge. I felt better after therapy—mainly because the therapist normalized my feelings. She explained that many new moms feel this way. She said that anger is a normal human response to adjusting to motherhood, especially as their child begins to enter the period of pushing boundaries to gain autonomy. She reiterated the value of my tools: using breath and mantra, or affirmations.

That week, I reached out to one more person, my spiritual advisor. She suggested that I start explaining things to Harper. Rather than just putting up a gate and saying, "Don't go up the stairs," I needed to explain the reasoning. She said, "Harper wants to know why," From then on, I started explaining everything to Harper. Instead of grabbing Harper off the swing and putting her in the stroller to leave the park, I explained, "Harper, we're going to get off the swings in three minutes. We're going to get in the stroller to go home because it's getting late. It's dinner time, so we're going to go home to eat." "Harper, please don't climb the stairs. If you climb the stairs, you could fall and get hurt. Mama doesn't want to see you hurt." This form of communication helped dramatically. The mini tantrums became fewer and farther between. Within weeks of the initial hippopotamus grunting, terrifying, stair episode; I found myself on the other side of mom-rage. Sure, I still have moments where I find myself impatient or peeved, but that's what it is to be human. Turns out, being filled with rage is also human.

Harper: thirteen months old

One of the great loves of my life is currently two feet tall. She knows seven words. The one she says most frequently is my favorite to hear…mama. She giggles when other people laugh, she rolls around in blankets in total ecstasy, and slides down stairs on her belly. Right now, for a brief moment in time, I have the great honor of being the most important person in her life. One day, a day that will probably come sooner than I can imagine, she will have her own great loves. Apart from me. There will likely be seasons where she will not consider me a great love. I'm prepared for the age of fifteen when she barely even likes me. She'll tolerate me. But we'll get past that. My big wish is that I'll be, alongside her dad, her steadiest love. The person she calls to share the mundane, the good news, and bad. The person she calls when she has a flat tire, scores well on an exam, has her first crush, and experiences heartbreak. My wish is to know the names of her friends, her biggest fears, and her wildest dreams. To be privy to such insights would be a gift. These experiences are years away, but I know they start now. In little ways. I know that by asking her about her favorite colors, responding to her incessant, "mama, mama, mama"s, and singing to her while we put on her shoes, we are thickening the invisible chord that connects us. Today and forever.

CHAPTER 16

Aging

My brothers, sisters-in-law, Brian, and I were sitting around talking on Thanksgiving weekend. Harper was still an infant. For whatever reason—maybe there was a lull in conversation, or someone was deep in a monologue on topic I wasn't interested in—I zoomed into my brother's salt and pepper hair; I noticed the puffy bags under my husband's eyes. I also became suddenly aware of my deepening wrinkles. I may have interrupted whoever was speaking when I blurted out, "I feel like I've aged ten years in the last three months." Everyone agreed. Not that I looked older, at least that's not how I interpreted it, but that they too felt that parenthood expedited the aging process. We all jumped into the conversation: The girls started discussing their lack of sleep. The guys started chiming in on how they no longer have time to go to the gym. One brother started talking about the incessant worrying. And I had to air my grievances about not being able to get Botox.

This subject is frequently omitted, and as I'm writing about it, I can see why. It's uncomfortable to risk coming across as shallow, but I can't be the only woman who missed certain forbade treatments during pregnancy and early motherhood. Longing for Botox was, an albeit trivial, yet ever-present, part of my motherhood experience. It would seem disingenuous of me to skip it. As a person that practices natural medicine, I can imagine how counter-intuitive this admission may sound. But people are multi-dimensional; I can rub turmeric on my face AND use injections. I confess that by Harper's first birthday, I was motivated for her to start weaning. I wanted my body back! As adorable as Harper's little hands were, pulling my shirt down to get her meals, I was ready for my chest to be mine again. I was also eager to return to the treatment that softened the lines on my face.

Young mothers may have a different experiences. Some may welcome the way that being a mom matures them. I thought about my own mother; she gave birth to my brother and I, at ages 23 and 25, respectively. Surely, she went through her fair-share of minimal sleep, and constant worrying. But, because of her youth, her lines would stay hidden for at least another five years. I know that aging is part of life. I tried to embrace it. I practiced self-compassion and affirmations that helped lessen my concerns. My favorite affirmation comes from author, Louise Hay, "I love myself at every age. Each moment of life is perfect."

I confess, I Google searched: how to prevent wrinkles. One of the top results stated that reducing facial expressions such as big smiles can prevent fine lines. What a joke! My daughter makes me smile all the time. The best part of being a mom is having access to on-call reasons to be joyful. I'd sooner have a face covered in grooves than reduce my tendency to smile.

CHAPTER 17

Mental Health

"How's the baby?" This is the first question most people ask when a new baby is brought into the world. It's a fair question. Babies are after all, not only adorable, but they're vulnerable, and utterly dependent on adults to care for them. We're right to be concerned about babies. Though, the question that is just as important, and asked less frequently, especially beyond the initial few weeks of delivery, is "How's the mother doing?" In brief, I was a mess. From day one of motherhood, I suffered from insomnia. I slept, on average, a broken four hours a night, for about six months. I was on constant high alert. I responded to every little sound and movement in my environment, I sometimes imagined the sound of Harper crying, and responded to that as well. My mind was constantly racing with worst-case-scenarios and irrational fears. I was filled with self-doubt. My perception of my unpreparedness led me to Google every twenty minutes. Google is no place for an insomniac, high-strung person—at 3 AM, or anytime.

It was a case of the chicken, or the egg. I don't know if the insomnia created anxiety, or if the anxiety created insomnia. Either way, the two co-existed for upwards of six months. The wild thing is, I was going through all the motions as though everything was fine. I was caring for Harper—adoring her every move. Within months, I returned to teaching yoga at 6 AM while Harper slept near me. I was interviewing babysitters. Raya, our first babysitter, came for several hours, once a week. During those hours, I resumed my internship; I met with clients and my supervisors, and I met with my Ayurveda clients. I was present, holding space for people—but in some respects, I was a mere shell of myself. I was running on adrenaline and fumes.

I had friends over. We traveled to visit family. We celebrated two major holidays. Maybe I missed my calling as an actress, because it's fascinating to me that no one noticed or expressed any concern. I was after all, in school for clinical mental health counseling. I was surrounded by professionals trained in the art of evaluation. My mind was jammed packed with knowledge of the DSM-5. The symptomology of mental health disorders were cataloged in my brain. I met with my professors and supervisors weekly, and no one flagged my affect or behavior. Apparently, I was faking being okay so well, that I didn't even recognize how imbalanced I had become. I figured all moms experienced unprecedented anxiety; I presumed that no new mom slept through the night. I normalized the abnormal.

My case of postpartum anxiety went undiagnosed, and untreated. It wasn't until Harper was nine or ten months old that I fully realized I had been in a very rough space. I was sleeping in healthier three to four hour stretches, waking only to nurse, then drifting back to sleep. My nerves gradually settled, and the tension slowly left my body. It took feeling better for me to realize how bad I truly felt. While pregnant, I prepped myself for the potential of postpartum depression. I knew the signs. I preemptively decided that should I suffer from PPD, I would seek treatment. I would see a counselor, and take medication if necessary. I knew that I would do whatever I needed to do; I was not going to allow depression to rob me of my much-anticipated joy of motherhood.

Postpartum anxiety, on the other hand, was not on my radar. It is the lesser talked about postpartum disorders. It is standard for new mothers to take a PPD inventory every time they visit the pediatrician with their baby. I was not, however, screened for postpartum anxiety. I found the condition perplexing because I was functioning, and I was not unhappy, per-say. To the contrary, I was in a state of euphoria— I was totally in love with my daughter, and elated to be a mother. Especially at first, I found the duties of caring for my baby to be fulfilling. PPA was not ostensibly negatively impacting my relationship with my daughter. I felt very connected to her; and we were bonding.

Without my knowing, though, postpartum anxiety was affecting ME. I found it difficult to concentrate. I was making unnecessary errors, even silly ones like getting in the shower with my socks on. I wasn't nourishing myself well; I fell underweight. Mood-wise, I enjoyed alone time with Harper, but I struggled socially. I could only maintain composure for a limited amount of social engagement, beyond that, I was faking it. I remember, after a particularly long day, I was being short with my husband. He said, "What's wrong? You seemed fine all day?" I responded through tears, "I was faking it. Do I have to fake it with you too?" Poor Brian... It's the people closest to us who are bestowed with the fortune and burden of seeing the truth of who we are. I wasn't unhappy. Rather, I was completely depleted.

In retrospect, I could have forecasted my experience—I have a history of anxiety and interrupted sleep. I wish I had been better prepared. I wish education and resources were made abundantly accessible to all new mothers. I am not a doctor, professor, or politician. I do not have a strategy for how to improve mental health care for new mothers on a systemic level. What my experience gave me, however, is the awareness that there is a gaping hole in this space. We, as mothers, need to have more conversations about our mental health. I see why the idiom "It takes a village," has been repeated billions of times. Historically, babies were raised by a tribe of mamas, aunties, grandmas, and neighbors. Taking care of babies was a community effort. Nowadays, many women, I'll speak for myself—try to do it all. Alone. If I were to do it again, there's one thing I would adjust. I'd ask for help…and, I'd accept the help.

CHAPTER 18

Redefine Identity

dentity is a funny thing. Perhaps there are people who enter the world with a sure sense of self. Through school years, and into adulthood they maintain an understanding and acceptance of who they are and what they're here to contribute. I was not one of those people. There's no need to go into the extensive depths of trials and tribulations that led me to who I've become, but suffice it to say, I went through my fair share of growing pains before establishing a healthy sense of self. I was loved as a child. I felt comfortable in my skin. Puberty was rough. I lost and abandoned myself. I spent my twenties crafting my identity—I traveled, learned about spirituality, found what I was passionate about, and tested my heart through eye-opening relationships. I finally settled into my "self" in my thirties. I curated my life to match the ideals I held dear. It took decades to arrive, but I was finally secure in my identity.

Overnight, my identity became destabilized; my primary roles, how I saw myself, spent my days, and interacted with people, all changed. I felt like my identity, the one I worked so hard to create, had been obliterated. All of my previous values and priorities were minimized by my new priority—care for Harper; keep her happy, healthy, and safe—nothing else matters. Becoming a mother was instantaneously all-consuming. Somewhere in the continuous cycle of feeding, changing, cleaning, and soothing, I temporarily lost myself.

For the initial eight weeks of my daughter's life, I relinquished all of my priorities outside of caring for my new baby. I didn't teach yoga, meet with clients, or work towards my graduate degree. I had very little variety in my daily routines. The time and energy I would have otherwise invested in these identity bolstering outlets were replaced with a singular focus. Mothering. My new identity was entirely predicated on how well I cared for my daughter. I did this at the sacrifice of my healthier sense of self. Temporarily, I became a martyr. I slipped into a precipitous mindset— *If being a mom is all of who I am now, I better do it perfectly, and without interference or help.* Behaving like a martyr was a betrayal to my whole self. It emptied me. It's no wonder I didn't feel fulfilled.

Sure, I was infatuated with my daughter; caring for my baby was my dream come true. Although mothering gave me a sense of fulfillment, I felt unfulfilled. Various parts of my life, to which I attached my identity, had been put on pause. I had zero alone time. I realized I was missing myself. Being independent has always been the paramount feature of my identity. I backpacked Europe alone. I lived in India alone. I took myself on solo dates to the movies, and I found solace in long walks in solitude. As a new mom, I was singing nursery rhymes while shampooing my hair; I couldn't even shower alone. I felt like my freedom was gone. I felt like my identity was gone. And I felt extremely guilty for feeling that way.

For the first seven to nine months of Harper's life I was so absorbed in motherhood that I resigned myself to the fact that the "old me," was dead. In retrospect, that perspective was dramatic and shortsighted. As Harper grew, I was able to delegate caretaking responsibilities; Harper started daycare— which was a huge game changer in terms of me feeling like myself again. Once Harper was in daycare and sleeping through the night, I was able to refill my energetic fuel tank. I learned that new motherhood, and the experience of being in constant fight or flight, dysregulated my nervous system—that was a big reason I felt disconnected from myself.

In time, I found the space to ground myself and reconnect. I realized I get to be a devoted mother AND I get to be all the other things that fulfill me. I am not suggesting, by the way, that anyone else would share my same need to diversify how they spend hours in the day. If I did it again, maybe being with my new baby 24-7 would feel fully gratifying. We all need different things, at different times, to feel like ourselves. Identity is a malleable concept. I'm sure I'll go through several more iterations of me. One thing I know for sure is, being a mom will always be the most treasured piece of my identity.

Harper 11 months old:

You will never be alone again. I wish someone would have told me...

Every shower you take for at least the next year will be accompanied by the squeals right outside the glass door. You'll have a built-in sidekick for walks, doctor's appointments, grocery store runs, get-togethers with friends, and vacations, for the foreseeable future. There will be moments where you are spatially alone, but mentally, the baby will be there. You'll be thinking about if her crib is safe for sleeping, if the temperature in their room is set to a comfortable degree. You'll be wondering if they're okay, if they miss you, if they need anything, or when you'll be summoned back to duty. You may find moments of solace to close your eyes, watch HGTV, or read a book, but even then, you will not be alone; you'll have the baby monitor notifications turned on, your ears will be open, and you'll be waiting for the signal— the call to duty. Being a mother as I have learned is a constant position. Ubiquitous in nature. Settle in.

CHAPTER 19

Babies Have Opinions

I was under the assumption all babies entered the world with proclivities for the same two things—sleep and milk. I also presumed that all babies liked pacifiers and bottles. I've seen enough cartoons to know that when babies cry, bring their tiny fists to their faces, and enormous tear-drops spray from the corners of their eyes. Cradles, bottles, and the sound of whaa,_whaa,_whaa—what a farce. I quickly learned that even before their personalities fully blossom, babies are equipped with preferences. Who knew a creature who was less than a month old would already hold opinions?

My sister-in-law shared her torment around her daughter's refusal to sleep with me. She tried all the usual methods; rocking, shhhh-ing, swaddling, and singing...nothing worked. "It took me six months to figure out that she just wanted to be left alone in a dark room", she discovered. If my niece, who was an infant at the time, could have talked, she would have said, "Get out of here; leave me alone. I'm trying to sleep." My daughter was the exact opposite. For her, cuddles and closeness were a prerequisite for slumber.

I gathered from my years of watching TV shows and movies that if a baby was crying, you could give them a pacifier and they would be, well, pacified. Unfortunately, his is not always the case. My daughter never took a pacifier. There was a period where she would only keep a pacifier in her mouth, while she was sleeping, and if I manually held it in place for her. Otherwise, she wouldn't take it. For us, a pacifier was a useless resource. The same went for bottles. Harper would only accept milk if it was dispensed from a warm body with a heartbeat...also known as, her mom. I have memories of giving my little brother bottles. I certainly gave bottles to my nieces and nephews. But for Harper, the experience of drinking milk had everything to do with the vessel it came in.

Harper liked to sleep while moving, so I thought I could get her to sleep in the swing. I tried and tried, but to no avail. Then one day while we were visiting my mom, Brian and I went on a walk. When we returned, Harper was fast asleep in the swing. "What!? How did you get her to sleep in the swing?" I asked. I was astonished. Pointing to the part of the apparatus where you can adjust the direction, my mother said, "She likes it to swing in this direction." My mom had adjusted the orientation, and she was out in seconds. "Remarkable," I thought. I was clear that Harper came out of the womb with preferences, and her opinions grow more pronounced by the day.

The phrase I hear most often now is, "Harper do". Harper has an affinity for wanting to try things herself. Like her mother, asking for help does not seem to be her first instinct. Respecting my daughter's preferences is helpful because it keeps her calm. However honoring a babies' opinions can also be taxing. On occasions when we're in a hurry, I'll want to carry her downstairs to expedite our departure, but she'll insist on walking—and each step feels painstakingly slow. But, in those moments I remind myself that her strong mind, will, and capacity to assert her opinions are the exact traits I want women to embody.

When Harper was tiny, her preferences were cryptic, and would often take me weeks to figure out. (And, they're constantly changing—might I add). As she has grown, she can communicate her choices more effectively. Sometimes, she clearly has a strong opinion, but lacks the vocabulary. When this happens, she gets super frustrated, then I try not to get frustrated, then we decode together. Understanding that babies are small people, and God knows, people think differently and want different things has been a valuable lesson for me. The process of figuring out what my daughter wants and needs continues to require a lot of patience, but I try my best because I want her to know that her opinions matter. I can not begin to write about parenting, because I feel like I am only ten minutes into motherhood. We haven't even approached the "terrible twos," or potty training, let alone the challenges that come with academia, and dating. But, I can already tell parenting a powerful little human is going to be a dance. On one hand, I want my daughter to know her voice matters, on the other hand, I cannot cave when she wants to bring all seven stuffed animals into the grocery store.

CHAPTER 20

Constantly On

There are certain conflicts one wouldn't even think to consider. For instance, what does a new mom do when an urgent need to defecate coincides with her daughter being attached to her chest, mid-nurse? I experienced such a dilemma, so I can tell you—the, said new mom, keeps the baby latched, heads to the bathroom, and poops while breastfeeding. Being a mother is constant; a round-the-clock job often lands us in less-than-ideal situations.

Harper was nine months old. I'm not sure what illness I had, but every symptom was present; chills, fever, weakness, nausea, and diarrhea. It was rough. It was midnight when my phone alerted to indicate Harper's baby monitor sounded. She was apparently awake and hungry. I felt woozy when I got out of bed, but figured I could nurse her, and fall back asleep. When I leaned over to pick her up from her crib, I threw up all over her bed. Still nauseous, I wiped up what I could with diaper-wipes before plopping down on the rocking chair to nurse her back to sleep. I laid her to rest directly on my pile of vomit and went back to bed. I was too sick to care. A few hours later, Harper signaled that she needed me again. The need for mommy proceeded all day. For twelve hours, I remained sick, and my sweet little girl crawled around following me from soft surface to soft surface, resting next to me to play, cuddle, and nurse. I was too faint to properly stand. I changed her diapers on floor. I used to savor sick days. I cancelled my meetings, laid in bed— binging on Netflix and enjoying mid-day dreams. New moms are not granted such luxuries.

Recently, though, I was sick and had the glorious honor of dropping Harper off at daycare. I returned home, slipped into bed, and slept for six hours straight. When I picked Harper up, I was able to communicate, "Mommy feels a little sick. Can you please be patient with me? I don't have much energy." She seemed to have understood on some level. My cold lasted all week. I broke my "no screen time after school" rule. Everyday after daycare, Harper and I cuddled-up on the living room floor with all her puzzles, toys, and books. *Cocomelon*, a show for babies that every parent will love and hate, played in the background. Each time I blew my nose, Harper took a tissue and went down the line, blowing the noses of all her stuffed animals and baby dolls. While I was still on-duty as mother, this was a welcomed improvement from the prior "sick day" I described.

I can't say there's any one aspect of motherhood that's hard, per-say; what makes motherhood difficult is the constant nature of the job. When my daughter was tiny, I felt my entire life was wrapped around satisfying her needs. I was honored to care for her, but I kept wondering, *will I get a break?* I remember calling my sister-in-law one day while feeling particularly haggard. "It gets easier," she said. I figured that was just a platitude people extended to struggling moms. My daughter is still young, so I am no expert in the long-game of motherhood, but I can already feel the shift. Being a mom will be a constant and permanent fixture in my lifestyle, but I anticipate the day will come when it's no longer as consuming. One day, my daughter will be grown, and I'll be longing for her to call and say she needs me.

CHAPTER 21

Changing Body

I slathered myself in oil. "Don't forget to do your breasts," my mother said. Through the powers of moisturizing or luck, I avoided stretch-marks. Well, my hips were graffitied in them for months, but they faded. My nipples, however, are another story. By the time Harper was ten or eleven months, she was performing downward-facing dog, and gymnastics on and around me while feeding; and tugging on my nipples. I probably should have put a stop to it, but I found it funny. My nipples did not—and will never be the same as a result. In addition, I still tinkle when I sneeze.

There are things about my body that will never be the same. Mainly, the way I think of it. I used to think of my body as this vessel that was entirely used for my purposes. I used to enjoy food, hop-scotch around the globe, and contort into intense yoga positions. There was also a period in my life when my relationship with my body was complicated and dysfunctional. For years, I manipulated my body through extreme diets and exercise, and I over-identified with it to the point that the way I felt about my body would determine my moods, and affect my self-esteem. Thankfully, by the time I got married and was pregnant, I reconciled those issues. I respected my body and tried to take good care of it, but I was still viewing it as mine, and mine alone.

Once pregnant, I realized my body was a container for two. In such, I was even more willing to allow it to stretch far beyond what I would have previously deemed acceptable. I welcomed my ballooning waist and widening hips. I felt womanly. I felt like the growth was evidence that a healthy baby was growing inside me. Even little kids know that pregnant women have big bellies; I fully anticipated that, but throughout my pregnancy I was fascinated by some of the lesser discussed features of a pregnant body. Within weeks of gestation my boobs were tender, and within months my areolas were large and three shades darker. Around month six, a dark purple line appeared on my body. It looked like someone took a paintbrush and just swept a line from my bellybutton to my vulva. The hair on my head stopped shedding when I washed it or combed it, and I was producing more earwax in a day than I normally would in weeks.

It's staggering to think that historically, maternal death was not uncommon. I feel so lucky to live in a time when child-birth is much safer and nearly always produces happy homecomings. But child-birth is still a raw and rough experience. After seventeen hours of labor, the final hour being high-stakes due to the umbilical cord being caught around Harper's neck, my daughter arrived. The doctor's felt a sense of urgency, so they used a vacuum— a suction used to move the baby through the birth canal and gave me an episiotomy—an incision to create a larger opening of the vagina. The vacuum didn't hurt the baby, and the stitches dissolved within weeks, so those events left no physical record. Childbirth, however, definitely left a lasting mark on how I appreciate my body. It's more than just a container, our bodies house precious human life.

Brian was very involved in the birthing process; truthfully, more than I probably would have liked. When I envisioned my birth-story, I imagined my husband standing near my face, holding my hand while I eloquently pushed our little baby of my body. One sweet bead of sweat would fall down my cheek, and we'd both wear serene smiles on our faces as our family went from two to three. That was not how it went at all. He was there when the nurse inserted a catheter into my urethra. Throughout the process, monitors constantly beeped, signaling if my heart rate, or Harper's heart rate, were in peril. Nurses recruited Brian to hoist me into various positions that somehow satisfied our hearts, literally. I had tubes hooked to my wrists and coming out of my vagina. I was bare naked, wearing nothing but a sweaty hospital gown. There was blood everywhere. Up until the final few pushes, when I was holding my own feet, Brian and a nurse held my legs as I grunted like a wild animal. I have since asked Brian how that experience affected him. He expressed that it was an out-of-body experience for him. He needs to write a book; I'd love to understand a man's perspective more fully, but I gather that he was able to isolate that event from how he normally sees me (from a naked perspective, at least). He has told me several times since, "You're one of the strongest people I know. I watched you deliver a baby." When I ask him if seeing me pregnant and giving birth has changed the way he sees me, he answers with the honesty I married him for— "I realized I used to objectify women. And I don't do that now." Brian's a noble guy. I think it's safe to say, he didn't objectify the female frame any more than I did. Culture teaches us that the female body is for sex and beauty. Becoming a mother teaches us that the female body is for so much more.

Twenty-Nine Weeks Pregnant

I looked in the mirror to see a faint purple line appeared overnight. It looked like I feel asleep with a paint brush in hand, and a dream caused me to twitch—sweeping pigment from my navel to my lady parts. I can't even see the line when I look down because my belly is ballooning more each day. I feel my body; swollen, inflated, and changing. And just when I'm about to make some unnecessary and false judgement, I remember this isn't about me. This is about you. This pure and joyous light that is incubating in the warm darkness of my womb. This is about you. This is about the preparation of you being revealed to planet earth as the incandescent being that you are. My being pregnant with you is one tiny, temporary piece of your abundant and radiant journey. So yes, I am growing as you grow. I'd be lying if I didn't say this feels deeply personal. On some level, indeed, this feels like it's about me. But baby girl, there's a reason the day a child comes into this world is not called Mother's Day. The day you're born is called your birthday, because this is about you. My role, along-side your daddy, is to; embolden your strengths, guide you, provide resources, nourish your body, warm your heart, listen to your ideas, show you acceptance, give you the freedom to be yourself, and saturate you with love. This is all for you. I have come to realize that there is one thing that grows even more than an expecting mom's belly—her heart. I love you.

Love,
Mom

~

CHAPTER 22

Pre-Baby Ignorance

I arrived at motherhood years later than many of my sisters-in-law and friends. So many wonderful women in my life were becoming mothers; I was adoring their kids, bopping in and out of their lives, and I was completely oblivious to the reality of their experiences. Now that I have the experience, I feel sorry that I was not as supportive as I could have been, yet I'm compassionate to the fact that I lacked the experiential context to know better.

Prior to having a baby, when I visited my friends who recently gave birth, I entered and instantly gushed over the new bundle of joy. I had no idea that my friend, the new mom, may have felt utterly invisible in that moment. As a new mom, it can feel like the baby is the star of the show, and you're an extra—barely relevant enough to receive a SAG card. I've since learned that get-togethers with a newborn can be challenging for a new mom. I remember the early months of new motherhood, friends and family members would come over for visits. I put on a smiley and happy front, but inside I was so exhausted that I was struggling to form coherent sentences. At the same time, I was wrestling with insecurities surrounding the interactions; my life had become so myopic; *I'm so entrenched in the rhythms of diapers and nursing, it's all I think about. Am I even interesting anymore?*

Prior to becoming a mother, I was also unaware of the sanctity of naps. When a friend declined an invite because the event was "during the baby's nap time", I would wonder, *why can't they just move the nap, or skip it all-together?* I learned that the baby's nap-time is as critical for the mom as it is for the baby. Nap-times provide a sacred pause for the mother—affording her a moment to shut her eyes, put her feet up, or do something that requires both her hands.

Leaving the house pre-baby was easy. It happened swiftly and often spontaneously. Now,I understand that a great deal of preparation proceeds every departure from home. I have a running check-list in my head; *do I have her diapers, wipes, sippy-cup, snacks, change of clothes, favorite toy of the moment that she'll freak out about once she realizes I've forgotten it, etc.* And that's just to run to Target. I now understand that if a mother is late, it may be that despite her best efforts and calculations, juggling more just takes more time. I am blown away by my friends with multiple babies—how they arrive anywhere on time is a triumph.

CHAPTER 23

Hormonal Woes

Hormones. What a journey.

When I was in my twenties, I suffered from severe PMS. When my capricious side appeared, some of the men I dated, often with the emotional intelligence of seventh graders, would say, "Is your period coming?" That comment infuriated me. There's nothing more condescending than someone invalidating one's feelings by chalking them up to hormones. With that said, when it comes to my pregnancy experience, I can attribute at least some of my own mood swings to hormonal imbalances. Throughout my life, I have become accustomed to my hormonal patterns; I've developed the ability to loosely predict how my they will affect me at various times of the month. But for me, pregnancy was this whole other experience. It was next level, and I was in uncharted territory.

During my first trimester, hormones caused relentless nausea. Pre-pregnancy, anytime my husband or I did something nice for one another, we would say "thank you" and the other person would say, "it's my pleasure." *Thank you for bringing me take-out. "It's my pleasure." Thank you for opening my car door. "It's my pleasure." Thank you for making the bed. "It's my pleasure."* We were newly in love, and that was our go-to pet-phrase. Fast-forward to the twelfth week of pregnancy; my husband watched the color drain from my face as I bolted to the bathroom feeling like I was going to puke. When I returned, I'd grab a saltine and tiny sip of water and tell him it was a false alarm. I'd reassure him I was fine. He said to me, "Thank you for going through this to grow our baby." I didn't have it in me to say *It's my pleasure.* It wasn't. For the sixteen weeks I was nauseous Instead. I said, *"It's my honor."*

My hormones went through another wave of adjustments during the second trimester. Somewhere around month three or four, I became uncharacteristically depressed. I cried for several days straight. I've been prone to feeling anxious, and of course, I've lived through sadness in my life. However, I've never dealt with unprompted sorrow. I reached out to my spiritual advisor for insight. She explained to me that my babies' karmas were being downloaded into her soul. She said that all at once, I was experiencing all the hardships and lessons my baby would experience throughout her entire life. She said that all pregnant women feel this, but because people don't understand, they think they're just being hormonal. She advised me to place my hand on my belly, and reassure my baby that she was loved, and would live a beautiful life. She also suggested that I place my barefoot on the earth for several hours to ground my energy. I was such a mess. I absorbed her advice. I was reluctant to share this newly discovered information with Brian because he's not into spirituality in the same way that I am. I was scared he would think it's all woo-woo, and that he wouldn't take it seriously. But I wound up telling him, because I felt too alone in my out-of-sorts-ness. I had to let him in. It should have come as no surprise to me that he listened to what I said without passing judgment. He supported me and held my hand while we walked barefoot on the beach for the rest of the afternoon. I don't know if it was the new perspective I gained from my spiritual advisor, Brian's support, the energy of the beach, or maybe a blend of it all, that healed me. But that evening, the depression lifted, and it didn't return. Towards the end of my second trimester, my hormones took me in a whole other direction. My libido went through the roof. I bought my first vibrator and used it more often than I care to admit.

My third trimester was all about nesting. I'm surprised they haven't coined whatever hormones are most dominant around week thirty-three through thirty-nine, the "nesting hormones". In the final few months before Harper came, I was fiercely determined to have every tiny article of clothing washed, folded, and hung. I was in the nursery, bent over with my huge belly putting together bookshelves, rockers, and swings until ten pm every night. I don't have a single handy bone in my body, but for two months straight I thought I was Bob the Builder, and Martha Stewart all in one. I wanted her environment and every piece of equipment in it to be set-up and beautiful. I installed her carseat and drove to three separate fire stations before finding one where they could certify its installation and safety. I was biologically driven.

I can describe my hormonal state during the fourth trimester to be nothing shy of a disaster. I felt like I was drowning in adrenaline and cortisol. I was anxious and insomniac. Undoubtedly, the lack of sleep was playing a part in my maladjusted endocrine system. Throughout most of my tenure nursing, I had zero libido. I had a baby attached to my chest for hours everyday. I felt like my body was more of a feeding station than anything else. I found comfort in an article I read; it stated that 95% of women who breastfeed full-time experience a decreased sex drive due to hormonal fluctuations. We produce prolactin to create breastmilk, and that reduces estrogen, which in turn lowers the libido. I'm sure plenty of women still crave sex even while nursing, but because I didn't, I clung to that article like a validating friend.

One upside of retiring from nursing was that my libido indeed returned. However, I suspect the hormonal shifts that came in response to the cessation of breastfeeding also played a huge part in my bouts of mom-rage. Gladly, everything seemed to return to baseline within about forty-five days. The month after I stopped nursing, my period returned. It was my first period in over two years, so I was concerned. Historically, I've had painful, debilitating periods. Shockingly, knock on wood, ever since having a baby, my periods have been regular and pain free.

I still am emotionally sensitive just before my period. I don't think this is a bad thing. In eastern medicine, there is the concept of Yin and Yang. Yin, is described as lunar, feminine energy. It is the energy of restoring and being. Our menstrual cycles are the ultimate in Yin functions—purely feminine. Its counterpart, Yang, is solar, masculine energy. It is the energy of being active and doing. We live in a very Yang culture; constantly incentivized to do and work. In Eastern Medicine, it is believed that when the energies of Yin and Yang in our lives are out of balance, we experience disturbances around our cycle. According to this theory, hormones are our teachers. Hormones do not create feelings, rather, hormones highlight the feelings we have that need attention. While it may feel like our hormones are taking us on roller coaster rides, I think we're fortunate to embody such powerful messengers. On one hand, hormones can feel like erratic inconveniences, but on the other hand, hormones give us access to a deeper, more subtle level of wisdom and awareness. I know now, more than ever, that when my emotions are heightened around my period, I need to look inward.

CHAPTER 24

Rejuvenation & Self-Care

'm of the belief that self-care is not a luxury; self-care is a necessity. Admittedly, my first year of motherhood did not reflect that philosophy. New moms are evolutionarily programed to focus on the baby at the expense of the self. In the beginning, I happily sacrificed my hygiene, sleep, and outside interests for my daughter. By month six, truthfully, I begrudgingly sacrificed my hygiene, sleep, and outside interests for my daughter. By month twelve, I was no longer willing to sacrifice myself. I realized that being a martyr wasn't good for me, and it wasn't good for our family. I was so invested in caring for my baby that I didn't tend to my needs as a whole-person, nor did I give my relationship with my husband adequate attention. I'm certainly not going to beat myself up over it. I was doing my best. I was just operating from a myopic perspective. My focus was all on Harper. After the one-year mark, I was able to zoom out and see the bigger picture. I needed attention, my marriage needed attention, and I was ready to shift focus.

Self-care is a tricky thing. First of all, there's no universal definition for the term. Self-care for some people translates to spa days, pedicures, facials, massages, and highlights. For others, it may mean taking a shower or talking with a friend. For other people, it's doing yoga, meditating, or sitting in nature. Self-care, for me, is a blend of all of the above. The heart of self-care is all about connecting with the self with the intention of replenishing energy. For me, I need to be alone to practice self-care. I've learned over the years, my energy is best restored when I exercise, spend time in nature, and read books. I have also learned that I am one of those people who requires copious amounts of self-care just to maintain a baseline. Meaning, to achieve the feeling of "normal," I need ample amounts of alone time, exercise, and sunshine. I knew that going into motherhood. I just didn't predict that caring for my baby would compete to strongly with caring for myself. I'm a huge proponent of self-care, and at the same time, I feel slightly icky writing this.

The part of me that feels icky is the same part of me that embodied the martyr. Somewhere in my mind I subscribed to the belief that being a good mom requires sacrifice. This is not true. I can care for myself and care for my daughter. This is not a zero-sum game. In fact, now that Harper is in daycare, and she's at an age where her dad can satisfy many of her needs as well, I am practicing sufficient self-care, and I feel myself to be a better mom for it. I show up for her with more energy. My perspective is clearer and more positive, and my temperament is more peaceful. She's too young to fully grasp it now, but

I am teaching her through my actions that investing in herself is important. I just know that without self-care, I am not a happy-healthy person. My lack of self-care at the beginning of Harper's life may have been a short-term necessity by circumstance, but I know that long term, self-care is a requirement.

The second item that needed addressing was my marriage. My relationship with my husband needed replenishing. Becoming parents is hard on a relationship. I only lived the experience through my perspective; at times I felt like I was doing so much more than he was, and I felt periods of aloneness and resentment. And at the same time, I can imagine that from my husband's vantage point, he was working extremely hard to support us, he was always asking how he could help, and his offers were being rejected. His wife's attention was concentrated on the baby, and he probably felt alone too. Luckily, we both understood that we were in a difficult chapter, that we were a team, and that we would eventually reconvene. But, our first year of parenting inarguably took a toll on us.

I found it difficult to give energy to my husband, because I didn't have extra energy to give. I remember my husband's birthday—Harper was eight months old, and she refused to nap that day. My mom was planning on watching Harper so Brian and I could go to dinner to celebrate. When 6PM arrived, I looked at him with a pathetic level of defeat. He knew I didn't want to go. He kissed me on the forehead and assured me it was okay by saying, "Another time." My tank was too empty to invest in my partnership. And that's a hard pill to swallow. But things got better. In sequence, Harper started daycare, I started practicing self-care; and my energy levels returned. Once I had energy, I found re-connecting with my husband to be not only possible, but finally, enjoyable. Relationship psychotherapist, Esther Perel, says that the best thing you can do for your kids is focus on marriage. I see a lot of truth in that. We're our daughter's primary model for how to be in a relationship, and I'd obviously like to set a good example. Brian and I have since charted out our rhythms for date nights and mini getaways. I feel rejuvenated, and as importantly, and not without hiccups, my marriage got the boost it need too.

CHAPTER 25

Good Enough Mothering

I entered motherhood with a lofty set of arbitrary rules and guidelines: My baby/child will not eat sugar. She will eat entirely organic. We will not introduce screens of any kind until the age of three. When at all possible, she will not see me using my phone in her presence. For me, these ideals worked in theory; in reality, they were completely untenable.

A few weeks into daycare, Harper's classmate had a birthday; the mom brought in cupcakes for the class. When I picked Harper up, she still had pink frosting hidden in the corners of her lips. This has happened many times since. I pack my daughter's lunch, but I can't control what she eats at school. And that's okay. Truthfully, I can't control what she eats at home either. Choosing what we put into our mouths is one of the first ways humans express autonomy. I can no sooner force Harper to eat organic strawberries and tofu, than I can force her to give me a hug. Luckily, she gorges in all of the above, but the point is—dietary mandates are not up to me. I can do my best, but my little one has preferences all her own. There are weeks where I exhaust myself—offering her every food option under the sun, and the only thing she'll eat is mac'n cheese. I respect her choice, and I've decided that has to be okay with me. Harper has experienced a few bouts of sickness, sore throats and such, where she can't stomach food. I see her little belly shrinking and I know she needs calories. I offer milk, toddler formula, the works—she won't drink it. So, what do I do? I give her sippy-cup after sippy-cup of apple juice. Loaded with sugar; I break my own rules. As moms, we have to be able to bend. We do whatever works.

I wanted to delay the use of screens as long as possible. At five and half months old, on a cross-country flight, Harper was getting restless. I found the animated movie, Boss Baby, on the airline's movie menu. She was momentarily entertained. I realized then that screens can be tools. Nowadays, Harper wakes up at 5:30 AM. We have three hours before school. You bet I use Cocomelon, the cartoon, as a tool. She sings and claps her hands to cartoons while I prep her breakfast and lunch, and answer emails. I have stayed committed to not using my phone around Harper, but she of course, is savvy to the device. We FaceTime her dad when he's away, and she requests that we look at pictures of "baby, baby" nearly every night. So, I solicit pictures of my nieces and nephews for Harper's viewing pleasure, and when she's memorized all of those, we Google pictures of random babies. We're not even two years in, and I have already compromised several of my "perfect parenting principles." I put that in quotes because there's no way that's a real thing. The parenting experts I respect the most will tell you, there's no such thing as perfect parenting—there's good enough parenting.

CHAPTER 26

Mom—Guilt

Harper was just shy of three months old when it was time for me to return to my internship and clients. I doubled down on my due diligence when it came to choosing a babysitter. Raya, the new babysitter, was as warm and gentle as they come. I emailed her a short novel the week prior to her start date, and I did all but laminate the excel spreadsheet I left for her on the kitchen counter. I explained, at-nauseam, in two separate formats, Harper's feeding and nap schedule, as well as how to rotate through sensory play activities and books. In retrospect, most of that was unnecessary.

I was doing everything I could do to feel okay about going back to work. I eased in; I would head upstairs to my home office, work for four or five hours, a couple days a week, and have my baby back in my arms before bath-time. Yet, for at least three months straight, until I got used to it, I felt a repeated surge of guilt wash over me every single time I left my daughter. I think guilt is an inescapable aspect of motherhood; It's like we're wired to feel it. I felt mom-guilt over the littlest things—Harper used to sit in her bouncer right outside my shower door. She had about eight-minute limit on being content without my presence. If, God forbid, I needed an extra two minutes to shave my legs, she would cry, and I would feel guilty. It gets more complex; there have been times when I'm on a date with my husband and I feel guilty for leaving Harper, AND I feel guilty for feeling guilty because the feeling of guilt detracts from our one-on-one time. Mom-guilt is layered and complicated.

The best piece of advice I received on reducing the feelings of mom-guilt is to expect it. Mom-guilt is unavoidable, so I learned to factor it in as a known feature in leaving my daughter. It seems counter intuitive, but by expecting to feel bad about leaving my daughter, when the time came, I felt less guilty. I first put this into practice when Harper was about four months old. My roots were five inches long and I desperately needed a visit to the salon. The sequence of events went as such; call salon and schedule hair appointment, call Raya and book her for the three-hour time slot—Day of; spend twenty minutes preemptively feeling bad for leaving, leave, and feel shockingly less guilty as an effect of planning on feeling badly. For the things we can't change, we learn how to cope.

CHAPTER 27

Blessings

I would be remiss if I did not directly acknowledge what a huge blessing it is to be healthy enough to conceive and deliver a healthy baby; let alone have the financial and social resources to raise a baby. Many stars had to align to make the last few years of my life possible, and the enormity of my good fortune is not lost on me. Part of me was tempted to shelf the release of this book because I didn't want my chronicles to come across as though I was throwing myself a pity party. Trust me, I'm not playing a tiny violin over here. The human experience is complex. We can simultaneously struggle and be grateful. Under no circumstances did any of my challenges overshadow the tremendous amount of gratitude I have for having the opportunity to experience the inevitable dilemmas that accompany motherhood. I have chosen to share my transparent and deeply personal experiences because I know other women can relate. My hope is that by exposing some of the less appealing aspects of the motherhood journey, other women will know they're not alone.

All experiences and adjacent feelings, big and small, are valid. I commonly hear my clients, who are mothers, discuss challenges related to child rearing, and then immediately invalidate their feelings by saying something like, "Oh, but I shouldn't be saying this, my sister struggles with infertility. I should just be happy I have a kid." Or "I feel bad for whining about never getting enough sleep; my neighbor's baby is still in NICU. My problems are nothing compared to theirs." There's value in keeping perspective; it is true that something can be comparatively small and subjectively big at the same time. But, if the narrative of new moms is 'suck it up and be grateful, other people are dealing with way worse,' we would be doing our collective wellbeing a disservice. Life doesn't exist without oxygen. I think giving our truths room to breathe is productive. We can generously presume the subtext behind every mother's grievance is: This is the most important job on earth, and I wouldn't trade it for anything.

CHAPTER 28

Baby Number Two?

My young niece and nephew were play-fighting in the back seat of my car while on a family vacation. I was eight months pregnant. "Guys, don't fight; show Uncle Brian how much siblings love each other, so Aunt Kristen can have another baby," I said, half kidding. I've gone back and forth on the idea of having multiple babies a million times. I have fond memories of growing up with siblings. As an adult, I'm grateful for my brothers, and I delight in being an aunt to their kids. Ideally, I've always wanted Harper to have a sibling, but many factors have complicated my mindset. For one, to put it lightly, I did not love being pregnant. Early on during my pregnancy, I thought that we would adopt our second. Throughout Harper's first year, I struggled with the idea of having another—*having one is so hard, how do people have two or more?* On Harper's first birthday my husband and I were emphatic in our decision for Harper to be an only child. I reasoned with myself, "*Harper can always marry into a big family, have those siblings, and be an aunt to their kids*".

Overnight, when my daughter was nineteen months old, my heart changed. I don't know if it was the pace in which I was watching my baby transform into a little girl—spouting new words by the day, and putting on her own shoes—or maybe it was my biological clock booming one last time. But, I officially had baby-fever all over again. There was a point in my first year of motherhood that I looked at pregnant women and felt pity for them. Then, the memories of my experience were still raw and amplified by sleep deprivation. Now, I see pregnant woman and think they look adorable! I feel excited for them, as well as hopeful for my future.

My husband and I talk candidly about our concerns; health risks, how growing our family will impact our marriage, and how to allocate our resources. We agree that if we try again, we'll need to move closer to family. I wanted to be an independent, super-woman the first time. But I have learned that well-supported women are superwomen too. I keep telling myself that part of the reason baby number one was so challenging was because I was crippled with anxiety. I now feel more informed and prepared in a way that only experience could have taught me. I don't foresee myself ensnared in anxiety provoked Google searches if we have baby number two. Experience has also taught me how transient each hardship was. Nausea doesn't last forever, sleepless nights don't last forever, strained marriages can be repaired…resilience is a beautiful thing.

I felt like going from zero babies to one was seismic, but I imagine that going from one to two babies will feel like a gentler change. I have never been one to allow fear to stop me from pursuing what I want. My mind has trepidations, my heart does not. If the course of my life has taught me anything, it's that the heart wins.

Kristen Lillian Riordan has a Master's Degree in Mental Health Counseling; she is an Ayurveda Counselor, Yoga Teacher, Wife and Mom. Kristen has been featured in Huffington Post, Yoga Journal, and Mantra Magazine. This is her third book, following— Your Life is Medicine: Ayurveda for Yogis, and Love Fearlessly: The Soulmate Within. She lives in St. Petersburg, FL.